HAUNTED
DUBLIN

D1615044

HAUNTED
DUBLIN

DAVE WALSH

First published 2008

Nonsuch Publishing
73 Lower Leeson Street
Dublin 2
Ireland
www.nonsuchireland.com

© Dave Walsh, 2008

The right of Dave Walsh to be identified as the Author
of this work has been asserted in accordance with the
Copyrights, Designs and Patents Act 1988.

All photos © Dave Walsh
www.davewalshphoto.com

British Library Cataloguing in Publication Data.
A catalogue record for this book is available from the British Library.

ISBN 978 1 84588 932 6

Typesetting and origination by Nonsuch Publishing
Printed in Ireland, by Betaprint

CONTENTS

AUTHOR'S NOTE

Haunted Dublin had barely reached the editor's desk at Nonsuch Ireland, and I was already under interrogation by friends and acquaintances, 'so … do you believe all this stuff?' It is, I suspect, a fair question – and the answer is 'no'. While it's well known that I've spent the last decade sporadically producing articles on bizarre topics, including UFOs and lake monsters, it still may not be clear that I eschew the shoehorning of phenomena into simplistic black and white, either/or, true/false, reality/ fantasy dichotomies.

However I *am* inclined to take a sceptical approach to the paranormal, but even the word 'sceptical' is often misunderstood – it means *critical*, rather than dismissive. While I would never spurn a story out of hand, I am entitled to ask questions, and to exist in a state somewhere between belief and non-belief, entertaining both premises equally. The poet John Keats defined this concept of 'negative capability' in 1817 in a letter to his brothers, saying:

> Negative Capability, that is when man is capable of being in uncertainties, mysteries, doubts, without any irritable reaching after fact and reason.

I have little doubt that *Haunted Dublin* will itself draw criticism – from the true believers' camp on one side, complaining that I'm too sceptical, and the ultra-rationalists on the other, telling me off for promoting gobbledygook. Well, they can feck right off, the lot of them.

Haunted Dublin does not claim that the ghosts it documents are 'real'; nor is it within the book's remit to prove that ghosts don't exist. Instead, I am more interested in celebrating the ghost stories of Dublin; what they tell us about the era in which they were recorded, about the people who experienced them, and about our own reactions, whether it be fear or laughter.

> The fate of all explanation is to close one door only to have another fly wide open.
> Charles Fort, *The Book of the Damned*, 1919.

In a sense, maybe all of the apparitions and creatures described *are* real. Not necessarily in a physical, measurable way, but by virtue of having become integrated into Dublin's urban folklore. Somebody, somewhere in this city believed, and continues to believe these ghost stories. Is *Haunted Dublin*, instead of merely documenting ghost stories, guilty of further proliferation? Probably. Folklore is not a thing of the past.

For hundreds of years, through generations of Dubliners, toe-curling tales have been passed on in

Dublin pubs, around fires, each one growing with the telling every time. Constantly re-engineered to suit their audience, and mixing in with Dublin's rich mythic web of history; Vikings, the Battle of Clontarf, the Norman invasion, the 1798 uprising, Robert Emmet, the 1916 Rising, the pages of the *Evening Herald*, last Monday's pub talk; and the overlay of deliberate fiction by the likes of James Joyce's *Ulysses*, Flann O'Brien, Brendan Behan and dozens of others, picked from the city's army of writers, each trying to connect with the soul of the city. Anyone who attempts to write a book proclaiming the non-existence of ghosts is, quite frankly, pissing in the wind.

It doesn't matter a damn if any of these ghost stories are true. On O'Connell Bridge, there's a plaque dedicated to a Father Pat Noise, 'who died in suspicious circumstances when his carriage plunged into the Liffey in 1919'. When it turned out that the plaque had in fact appeared as recently as May 2006, some members of Dublin's City Council wanted to replace it with something dedicated to a 'real person'. I found this terrifically amusing – this is a city that once had a public monument dedicated to *Anna Livia,* personified as a bronze statue of an improbably serene and ethereal woman on O'Connell Street, known more coarsely as the 'Floozie in the Jacuzzi', or the 'Hoor in the Sewer'. While an Anna Livia Plurabelle turns up as a character in *Ulysses*, and we're all very fond of Jimmy Joyce, I don't think we can claim that *Anna Livia* is a real person, any more than we can claim that Molly Malone, whose statue is a popular tourist attraction at the bottom of Grafton Street ('The Tart With The Cart'), existed outside the lyrics of a popular song. And don't forget that every year, on 16 June, Dublin officially celebrates the original Bloomsday, which although pinned to the year 1904, never actually happened beyond the pages of Joyce's *Ulysses*. Instead, 16 June 1904 was the date of Joyce's first romantic (and possibly erotic) outing with his future wife, Nora Barnacle. So much for reality.

For me, what is interesting about Dublin's stories – and in particular, *Haunted Dublin*'s ghost tales – is why they exist at all. Whether or not the paranormal events objectively happen in a real or measurable sense doesn't matter; the fact is, *somebody* has had the experience, and *somebody* was compelled to talk or write about it. It's possible that paranormal experiences involving the apparition of a loved one who has 'passed' may articulate a need for closure. Others situations seem stress related – many modern poltergeist stories involve troubled adolescents, or other family issues; whether these can actually manifest as physical poltergeist activity or are faked occurrences driven by personal issues is open to suggestion.

There's a rough pattern to many of the stories in *Haunted Dublin*, and in Irish ghost stories in general. Many of the tales that come from the 'big houses' tend to have a finale, backed up with a beginning that doubles as a dubious explanation. For example, a white lady is seen a castle A. She must have been the daughter/wife/sister of Lord B; she committed suicide, died of disease C or fell from a horse; her love for D is never consummated, thus she wanders the halls of her family mansion forever, seeking closure. These stories seem to have arrived through layers of romantic storytelling, often filtered via Victorian values or even Spiritualism. And there's often a moral to the cautionary tale, with some damned soul committed to an eternity in limbo for their crimes.

The ghost stories of Dublin's streets seem less clear-cut, more chaotic, and seem to be largely informed by an older, more rural form of storytelling that celebrates an absolute terror of the unknown, without looking for an explanation. *Haunted Dublin*'s tales of black dogs, black pigs, huge cats, suburban monsters with glowing eyes, and apparitions of goats seem to evoke the *Púca*, the terrifying shape-shifter of Celtic mythology. While the English *puck* comes across as merely mischievous character or prankster, the Irish *Púca*'s motives are obscure, and definitely more frightening. That said, an encounter with the *Púca* is rarely fatal, and is often instructive or helpful; at worst it will leave you confused, in a ditch somewhere.

I'm not saying that the *Púca*, Scaldbrother, the Dolocher or the Banshee are out stalking on the streets of Dublin at the moment. But that's no reason not to be scared.

TELL ME A STORY

Finally, I'm sure that *Haunted Dublin* will barely be on the shelves before I'll be asked, 'why didn't you put so-and-so story in', or emails will be coming in stating 'that story is WRONG, this is how it goes'. Well, please post all stories, updates, versions, complaints, abuse and threats on www.haunteddublin. com. Keep 'em coming – maybe we can produce *Haunted Dublin Volume II*!

ACKNOWLEDGEMENTS

I'd like to thank Ronan Colgan and Stephanie Boner at Nonsuch for all their help and guidance; Barry Kavanagh for the introduction and editing, and Damien DeBarra for his encouragement; All the ghost posters on p45.net, especially Roddy Peavoy, and Sean Carroll who sent me the Artane 'head without a body' story; Bernie Jameson at Today FM for relating her experiences of the haunted newsroom; 'Paul', the taxi driver who told me so many stories; Louis Parminter, Dean's Verger at St Patrick's Cathedral and his colleagues at St Patrick's Cathedral for their help, including my rescue from the cemetery after getting locked into it, and Terry O'Hagan at St Audoen's for the stories.

Dave Walsh
Dublin, August 2008

INTRODUCTION

The fact of the matter is that there are people in Dublin who say in all seriousness that they have seen ghost nurses and headless horsemen, and the whole pantheon of spectres that we'd expect in the pages of fiction. In this book you'll find that Dubliners also claim to have seen sinister bright lights emerging from the canal, and mysterious clouds coming through walls, and all manner of strange and terrifying phenomena. It's enough to make you sleep with the light on.

Most investigators into the paranormal, however, will tell you that *visual* apparitions are rare, and most ghost reports involve 'sensations' or 'sounds', rather like the creepy occurrences at Benburb Street and Hendrick Street recounted in this book. The problem for the investigator is how to interpret such data. In oral folklore, ghost stories tend to be more clear-cut: the sights and sounds are simply explained as being caused by spirits of the dead. But there is always the possibility that hauntings are caused by something else, whether that be an anomaly in the way humans interact with their environment, or hitherto unknown features of electromagnetism, or 'leakage' in the space-time continuum. I wouldn't hazard a guess myself.

It pleases me that the setting for these frightening scenarios is Dublin. I am a native Dubliner. I remember once during my schooldays a teacher asked all the boys to raise their hands if both their parents were from Dublin, and very few did; it seems the city has been full of blow-ins (like our Wexford-born author Dave Walsh) for quite some time. I don't know how far back my roots go; certainly my great-grandfather lived on East Road. Anyway, it takes a Dubliner to write an introduction to a book about Dublin, so here I am with my Dublin ghost story, which is a nice cosy one that should warm you up before Mr Walsh puts on the chill.

On a return visit from where I live in Norway to my native Dublin in 2007, I attended an extended family reunion, the sequel to a similar event thirty years before. This was my father's side of the family, associated with Sandymount. My mother hails from Terenure, although it's at Bohernabreena (see the chapter of this book that deals with 'the Hostel of the Red God') where you'll find my maternal ancestors buried. It's also on my mother's side you'll find distant connections with our mysterious ghost-botherer Walsh.

My father, Paddy Kavanagh, surprised the Kavanagh family gathering by providing everyone with a bound copy of a book he'd written specially for the occasion, mostly concerning his years growing up with his brothers and sister in a house on Tritonville Road, which the family occupied from 1929 to 1981. He was born in 1930 and left the house to marry in 1966. In his book I found much that he had never told me of these years. Of particular interest to us here was a page and a half about a ghost that dwelled in the house on Tritonville Road:

Miss Rhufethen was our in-house ghost in Tritonville Road. Whether she ever existed or not is immaterial. She may have been a ghost of conscience. Yet there were several occasions when I thought I saw her. Oonagh [his sister] occupied her room, but I never heard Oonagh speak of any spirit haunting her, day or night. Yet mother told me she was a real person, who died long before Uncle Dick, Aunt Katie, Bid and Paddy [the previous tenants], or our parents came to live at [the house].

She was a friendly ghost and frequented the landing just outside Oonagh's door. I never felt alone in the house, when I'd be there after school tending to the fire and bringing in fuel for the night to the dining room, which we used also as our living room, sitting by the fire and listening to the wireless. The rest of the house was freezing cold during wintertime. When no one else was at home I always felt I had friendly company.

The first time I saw Miss Rhufethen was on the evening I was sent to McAuliffe's Chemist in Sandymount for some messages. I can only remember one of the items I was to buy and that was Cuticura soap. I can recall that because of the method I used to remember it at the time – you get a cut and then you cura. Anyway, didn't I lose the 10/- note, which I was given to buy the goods and caused a National crisis with mother. I got a right leasadh teangain from her and was put to bed early in Oonagh's/Miss Rhufethen's room, which was the spare room at the time. I reckon that that must have been 1940, the time father's business was failing, due to war-time problems, and we were very short of money. In the midst of my tears I heard a kind lady's voice say 'don't cry Paddy, it will be all right!' I looked up and she smiled at me. I was appeased and fell asleep.

On another occasion I came home after playing in goal in a football match. I had hurt my back badly. There was no one at home at the time and having no house key, I had to climb over the back wall and get down into the lane. Then I had to break into the house. The agony of this exercise I can remember to this day. I made my way up the stairs and was gingerly turning the first landing when Miss Rhufethen appeared and gently helped me to my bedroom, saying she hoped someone would be home soon to help me to get a doctor. I lay down on my bed and almost immediately Jim [his brother] appeared asking how I had hurt my back. He gave me a crossbar, on his bike, up to Baggot Street Hospital, where I was told that I had strained the main muscle in my back. Some lotion was rubbed on the muscle and I experienced almost instant relief from the pain. I had to attend to have physiotherapy every day for a week. After the hospital visit I asked Jim how he knew I had hurt my back. He just said, 'Miss Rhufethen told me.'

Later, when coming home late after a night's devarsion, I would see her friendly face on the landing, head to one side with a quizzical smile on her face, asking the question what have you been up to? I'd smile back and wish her goodnight! I often prayed for her that she would rest in peace and yet I never wanted her to leave. I wonder is she still there?

About a year after reading this, I asked my father if he had indeed *seen* the ghost. He was philosophical about it, shrugging and saying, 'I don't know if I did nor not', more or less implying that the passage of time, or even the weirdness of the experience, affects the memory. But he told me he was very sure of the *voice* of the ghost on his first encounter, and of the *touch* of the ghost on his arm, guiding him up the stairs, on his second. He was sure of the *presence*.

My father's book also attests to the Banshee's appearances in Sandymount (she's not often seen in Dublin), but I thought the Miss Rhufethen story was the better tale to share with you. There's nothing like getting a ghost story first-hand from the person who experienced the uncanny event! In this book, you'll get a taste of that from Mr Walsh's experience of an inexplicably odd room in Benburb

Street, and he also manages to get the essence of a second-hand story across, as he sits and chats with a spooked taxi driver. Of course, the book also concerns peculiar goings-on that span centuries, passed down to us from Dubliners long gone. Or are they gone at all?

Enjoyable as all these stories both new and old may be, I hope that the days don't return when the very idea of a murderer's ghost ('the Dolocher') induces social panic in the city, and that there are never again angry mobs roaming Harmonstown Road in the irrational hunt for a spectral bodiless head. When it comes to the supernatural, it seems our sanity is often in danger. With his selfish taste for a good tale, we have our author to 'thank' for digging up all this unsettling stuff.

The scribbler conventionally known as Dave Walsh, an apostate mason, a ship's apothecary and a self-confessed owl-worrier, who has gone by many names (Dr David Fleschwood, Ignatius Rhapscold, Absinthius McIvoe, 'Sea-eyes' Catrill, the Knave de Zuela and many others), I have seen up close only once, at a Halloween dinner in Killakee House (see the chapter on the Hellfire Club). Here is a man who, one senses, has felt the crossing 'twixt this world and the next. A man with the haunted look of a widower, or a hangman. A man given to hours of morbid contemplation in the ruined castle that he inherited from his great aunt Emmeline. Here he comes with a swift gait, all dressed in black, swinging his swordstick. There is no better guide to come and take you by the hand and show you haunted Dublin.

Barry Kavanagh
Co-editor, Blather.net

THE HELLFIRE CLUB AND THE
GHOSTS OF KILLAKEE

Perched atop the Dublin Mountains, in the parish of Rathfarnham, is a 300-year-old ruined hunting lodge, its eyeless sockets of windows looking balefully down on the urban sprawl below.

Known as the Hellfire Club, it sits 383m on top of Montpellier Hill in an area called Killakee. Today it is a Sunday afternoon hill-walking destination for hardy families, and an illicit summer drinking venue for the suburban youth. Teenagers seem to be drawn there by the building's dark reputation and a noctural visit to the Hellfire Club has become a rite of passage. With reports of satanic rituals, an eighteenth-century appearance by the Devil and 1960s reports of massive black cats, who can blame them? Judging by the number of comments posted onto my website's Hellfire Club pages, the mythology of Montpellier Hill enables people to scare the bejasus out of themselves, and contribute to a rich Dublin oral tradition that borders urban gothic and rural folklore.

In fact, for city dwellers, the entire expanse of the Dublin hills probably seems a sinister place. Beyond the last streetlight it becomes a kind of liminal zone – not really country, but too wild and unknowable to be suburban. It is a place *in between*. Hikers, lashed by squalls, are forced to dodge deep bogholes while still in sight of the city. At night, the forest car parks are illuminated by the fogged-up windows of parked cars, obscuring couples engaged in the things that lovers do, while further out, hooded teenagers burn out stolen cars for entertainment.

Remnants of ancient megalithic structures dot the landscape, along with ruined and apparently haunted buildings, overgrown estate gardens and monuments to Civil War executions. It's no surprise that stories of weird goings-on retain a foothold in the Dublin Mountains.

Back in the 1980s, I was sometimes packed off to spend some of my school holidays with relations on the edge of the sprawling housing estates of Tallaght, Co. Dublin. Where they lived is no longer the city frontier – the suburbs have travelled on, steadily creeping up the Dublin mountains, towards the plantation forests and farms, towards the Hellfire Club.

One of my older cousins seized any opportunity to wind me up with scary stories. Coming from a quiet part of rural Co. Wexford I wasn't afraid of the dark, but there was a suburban edginess to his

'The Hellfire Club', the spooky hunting lodge in the Dublin Mountains, home to eighteenth-century 'divilment' of the highest order.

tales that was both fascinating and completely alien to me.

At night, with our heads stuck out the window of his attic room, we would gaze at the eerie silhouette of the Hellfire Club. It reminded me of an empty skull. In reality, my cousin was as intent on scaring himself – he did have a penchant for horror movies, a poster of Hannibal Lector on his bedroom wall, and an artistic tribute to Ted Bundy downstairs. I'm still amazed that he turned out relatively normal.

The stories he told me were exciting, if somewhat vague, involving a secret society at work in the mountains. They involved a kind of Irish Klu Klux Klan/Hammer House of Horror crossover, with bonfires and ritual executions of cockerels on Halloween. I was told that their torch-lit processions could be seen on a clear night from the housing estates of Tallaght. When I finally fell asleep it would be to visions of malevolent miscreants in white hooded robes running pell-mell around the Dublin hills. Part of me was sceptical – how could this be going on, *in this day and age*? The rest of me, of course, wanted it to be true, and couldn't wait to spy on these devil worshippers in action.

One Sunday, my aunt and uncle took us for a drive up the hills – and for a walk to the Hellfire Club. The car park today has a standard Coillte (Irish state forestry company) sign that simply reads 'Hell Fire Wood', although as of 2008, most of the atmospheric plantation forest has been stripped away, ruining the effect somewhat.

We climbed up the curving forest road, and then detoured onto a steep incline. Before us lay a huge rock, which my cousin tried to persuade me was the altar, used for regular satanic blood sacrifices – he even pointed out some worn red paint stains as evidence of blood. I was sceptical, but intrigued. Wouldn't any self-respecting Satanists carry out their rituals on top of the hill, rather than halfway up, in a bunch of trees? Where was their commitment, their sense of drama?

Reaching the top of the hill, the Hellfire Club comes into view, in the middle of an exposed clearing. There seems to be something both mysterious and repulsive about the ruin. Apart from a few minor portholes and arrow slits, all of its major windows face north-east, towards the city. After 300 years of exposure to the elements, it's in a state of surprisingly good repair, even though a bonfire was lit on the roof during Queen Victoria's visit to Dublin in 1849.

The interior of the lodge has been made safe for public visits, presumably by Coillte, with concrete stairs, and iron safety rails across the windows. Entering through the low front door, via a small windowless porch, there's a hallway. On either side, there are two large low-ceilinged rooms, with fireplaces, and a low room to the rear. Upstairs is the same layout but with much higher ceilings. The walls are damp and green with mould, making tough work for local graffiti artists. Thick mud covers the floor, mixed human detritus left behind by the revelries of cider-drinking teenagers. Outside, at either end of the building, there are another two large side 'sheds' with doors much higher than the lodge stables, perhaps.

On this first visit, as a child, I was motioned towards a tiny room on the lower floor – this was, I was told, where the Devil himself had appeared. According to the legend, a mysterious stranger sought shelter at the lodge in the wee hours of a stormy night. Over supper, one of his hosts dropped a fork (or in some versions, a playing card) beneath the table, and on bending to retrieve it, noticed that the traveller had a cloven hoof. Their scream of horror roused the Devil into a fury, leading him to exit the room through the ceiling, in a ball of fire.

This unlikely tale is a bit of a portable legend – I first heard it in connection with the haunting of the desolate nineteenth-century Loftus Hall, on Wexford's Hook Peninsula. In that version, the comely and marriageable young daughter of the house, distracted by her flirtation with the handsome young traveller – who, of course arrives during a storm – drops her playing card, and encounters his cloven hoof. Once again, he vanishes in a thunder-clap leaving a brimstone smell behind him, and apparently doing terrible damage to the ceiling. The Devil certainly got around in those days.

Back at the Dublin Hellfire Club, there were stories that during a 'black mass' a footman reportedly slipped on a mass of drunken bodies lying on the floor and spilled a drink on the coat of Hellfire founder Richard Chappell Whaleyt, who in turn poured brandy upon the man, set him alight, and soon had the entire building ablaze. Most were too drunk to escape. It's difficult to ascertain how much truth there is in these stories. But where there's smoke …

The Irish Hellfire Club is known to Dubliners now as a building in the mountains, but the club actually refers to a select group of powerful society figures. Through association with members of the club, the name transferred to the structure on Montpellier Hill. The term 'hellfire club' is somewhat generic – in the early eighteenth century, it was a term used to describe any band of moneyed urban wastrels, who spent their time drinking, duelling and generally raising hell on the streets of London, Dublin and other cities. Today's equivalent would be the stag parties and groups of otherwise respectable and well-dressed 'lads' who get together for drinks, and end up getting out of control. A Royal Edict was passed in 1721 condemning, 'young People who meet together, in the most impious and blasphemous manner, insult the most sacred principles of our holy religion, affront Almighty God himself, and corrupt the minds and morals of one another', which sounds like a contemporary Saturday night out in Dublin.

Seemingly founded by first Earl of Rosse Richard Parsons and Richard Chappell Whaley in 1735, the Irish Hellfire Club apparently lasted about six years. It should be noted that there's no evidence that the group ever called itself the *Hellfire Club* …the title probably stuck later on. Parsons, according to writer Peter Somerville-Large in *Irish Eccentrics*, was a 'sorcerer, dabbler in black magic … and a man of humour and frolic' – a demeanour undiminished by illness. As he lay at home on his deathbed on Dublin's Molesworth Street, a local clergyman – the rector of St Anne's – wrote to him begging him to 'repent of his evil ways'. Rosse read the letter with some amusement, and on noticing that it simply began 'My Lord', resealed it and addressed it to Lord Kildare, who was famous for his 'piety and integrity of life'. The poor man received a terrible grilling before the truth emerged, but by then, Rosse had presumably departed to a far hotter place. The Hellfire Club seems to have been disbanded following his death in 1741.

Richard Chapell Whaley (father of the infamous rake Buck Whaley) was known as 'Burn Chapell' due to his Sunday morning habit of setting fire to thatched Catholic churches. Also involved were Lord Santry, Simon Luttrell the Sheriff of Dublin (responsible for getting Dublin madame Darkey Kelly pregnant, and perhaps for the legacy of her haunting of St Audeon's church – see section on Dublin's Ghost Bus), and Colonel Jack St Ledger, who according to Somerville-Large's book *Irish Eccentrics*, was so obsessed with the Duchess of Rutland that he would drink the water with which she had washed her hands. The club seems to have been, for its time, sexually egalitarian – another Hellfire Club, or at least another branch, in Limerick city, listed a Mrs Blennerhasset as one of its more notorious members.

It seems that this motley band of libertines used two meeting places; the long vanished Eagle Tavern on Dublin's Castle Street, where they would swig *Scultheen*, a mixture of whiskey and rancid butter and the hunting lodge at Montpellier, now known as the Hellfire Club, although it is extremely unclear how common it was for the group to use this latter venue.

While constructing this hunting lodge in 1720, MP William 'The Speaker' Connolly apparently demolished a nearby stone circle and then used the uprooted menhirs as flagstones and lintels. Connolly was warned about the dire consequences of this desecration. 'Oh, now he's messed with things he shouldn't have,' muttered the locals – or so the story goes.

But sure enough, the roof blew off in a subsequent storm – or was it the Devil? Or God? Connolly, unwilling to be thwarted, rebuilt the roof – this time in pure stone, keying it like a bridge. Nearly three centuries later it is still intact, and while it doesn't exactly let in rain, the enduring damp has resulted in dozens of mini-stalactites suspended from the stone ceiling.

At some point, Connolly sold the building to members of the Hellfire Club, leaving the lodge to become associated with tales of card games with the Devil, ritualistic whiskey-drinking, drunken orgies of arson, and giant black cats.

There's the apocryphal story of a priest who, on stumbling across the Hellfire Club's fun 'n' frolics, was hauled inside by the drunken bunks, where he saw a huge black cat being tortured. Breaking free from his inebriated captors, the priest grabbed the cat and uttered an exorcism, which tore the cat to pieces and released a demon that shot up from its corpse. Hurtling through the roof, it brought down the ceiling and scattered the assembly.

One wonders why a priest was roaming around the top of Montpellier Hill at that time of night, or why the priest thought it was better for the cat to be ripped apart by the demon rather than the humans.

Other fragmented stories are associated with the building – there's mention of black masses, defrocked priests forced to perform parodies of the Catholic Mass, more sacrificial black cats, and even the murder of a dwarf.

Killakee House, Rathfarnham – home of Hellfire Club shenanigans, and haunted by a giant black cat, poltergeists and other strange phenomena.

THE BLACK CAT OF KILLAKEE

Down the hill from the hunting lodge, beside the car park (a dodgy enough place at night, and the site of a 1999 murder), is Killakee House, an eighteenth-century farmhouse, which operated as a restaurant during the 1990s, closing its doors to business around 2001. It now seems to be a private dwelling. At one point in the early twentieth century, it was allegedly used by Countess Markievicz (1868-1927), the Irish revolutionary and the first woman to be elected to the House of Commons. Five of her fellow IRA members are reported to have died in a gun battle at Killakee House during the War of Independence of 1918-21. I'm not sure how true this is, however it *has* been documented that in around 1907, Markievicz used another cottage at the east end of the mountains, near Lamb Doyle's pub, and during the 1916 Rising, the family of executed 1916 leader James Connolly stayed here.

In 1968, the Killakee House was opened as an art school by a Mrs Margaret O'Brien and her husband Nicolas – a retired Garda Superintendent. Before long the place was apparently beset by paranormal events. Oddly enough, Patrick Byrne, columnist for the *Evening Herald*, who would go on to publish the book *Irish Ghost Stories*, was invited to the centre's opening – possibly because of his status as a collector of paranormal folklore, or that he came from not too far away.

On moving in into Killakee House, Mrs O'Brien was informed by the local people that a massive black cat haunted the area, supposedly the size of an Airedale dog (about 60cm at the shoulder).

Her husband *did* claim to have seen a big black animal disappearing into the foliage one day, but didn't mention it to anyone until their artist friend Tom McAssey and two workmen were one night working late in the house. According to McAssey in the *Evening Herald* of 10 December 1968, a door seemed to open by itself – despite having earlier been locked with a six-inch bolt. Going out into the dark hallway they were confronted by a shadowy black draped spectre that said, 'I can see you. You can't see me. Leave this door open' in a 'low guttural' tone. Two of the men ran. McAssey stayed a moment, turned to run, but looked back and saw a horrible black cat with red glowing eyes staring at him.

McAssey later created an oil painting of the cat, which I first saw hanging in Killakee House in the 1990s, while it still operated as a restaurant. It's an odd painting – rather than looking like a wild animal, the painting portrays a rather annoyed and malevolent looking domestic cat curled up, as if by the fire. Val McGann, who lived in a caravan next to the house, claimed to have stalked the monster with his shotgun but, like everyone else, was unable to track it down.

Locals were sceptical, according to an article in the *Evening Herald*, on 29 April 1970; Mrs Joan Kelly, who had lived in Killakee House for twenty years said she'd never come across any 'queer things … of course we often hear the screeching of badgers or cats in the ditches in the night, but I know of no spooks around the place. I think the whole business is the figment of some person's imagination.' A Mrs Ann Doyle, a local resident for forty-two years, was quoted as saying, 'we live and work very hard here and we don't have time for ghost stories,' while her son John, 'I have lived here all my life, I slept in the Hellfire Club one night and did a tour of the whole place around to find out if these things did exist. It's a lot of blarney.'

Even musician, songwriter, TV personality and author Shay Healy was implicated. He told the *Evening Herald* that he regularly visited Killakee house. He was in the house at about 3a.m. when the lights startling flickering before finally going out at 5a.m. – hardly evidence of paranormal activity in itself, considering this was the late 1960s, in an old house up a mountain. Ironically, Healy later wrote a musical about rural electrification in Ireland called *The Wiremen*, so I suppose he should be considered something of an authority on the subject.

'There was continuous bell ringing and various other sounds', said Healy. 'We ran out the back and shouted to the so-called ghosts to come out, but nothing happened. It was very fascinating.'

More paranormal events were reported from the house, including apparitions of nuns, poltergeists, power failures during seances and mysterious ringing bells. At one point, a Catholic priest was apparently called in to sort things out, to no avail. Things got even dafter when headgear – in the form of small caps – were reported to be regularly 'teleporting' themselves into the house, and were found hanging on picture hooks or other odd places. In April 1970, newspapers reported a night of fierce poltergeist activity with broken furniture, cups and plates smashed. Another time, a '3-foot tall crippled man' appeared, before turning into a cat. Ghosts of nuns and a 'handsome Indian' were seen parading through the house.

In around the beginning of 1971, while plumbing work was underway in the house, a shallow grave was found beneath the floor, allegedly containing the skeleton of a dwarf and a brass figurine, depicting a horned and tailed devil thumbing its nose. Could this be the dwarf that the Hellfires are supposed to have murdered back up the hill at the hunting lodge? Some of the reports of the time challenge this, however, saying the skeleton was of a small child.

Some years ago, I organised a Halloween dinner at Killakee House restaurant, gathering together a dozen of so of my friends to celebrate Samhain high above the chaos in the city below. Sadly, no paranormal experiences were had during our repast.

THE HOSTEL OF THE RED GOD

A couple of years ago, while researching some Irish mythology, I discovered that a much earlier echo of the Hellfire Club myth in nearby Bohernabreena (*Bothar na Bruidne* – the Road of the Hostel), where the river Dodder ambles its way down into the city. According to an ancient book, *The Destruction of Da Derga's Hostel*, the river was once straddled by the *Bruiden Da Derga*, a magical hostel presided over by the rather sinister Da Derga, or 'Red God' – the god of the dead. Only those destined to die – or already dead – could enter the hostel.

Looking north-east from Bohernabreena, the Beltaine (May Day) sunrise appears over the rocky promontory of Howth. Looking back, the Samhain (Halloween) sunset vanishes behind Bohernabreena, with the Hellfire Club standing proud on the skyline. It was from Howth – in Irish *Ben Étair*, on Samhain night that the armies of chaos would scout forward from the sea, to attack the *Bruiden Da Derga*, which would be crowded with partying deities and warriors, a swine's head screaming upon the fire. *The Destruction of Da Derga's Hostel*, now included in the readily available *Early Irish Myths and Sagas*, goes into powerful detail about the gatecrashing of Da Derga's party. Perhaps the devil of the Hellfire Club was the Red God coming back. Perhaps he wanted to wreak revenge upon the invaders.

I'll leave you with a prescient quote from writer and critic V.S. Pritchett:

I was brought up on the legend that the sinister little ruin on top of the Dublin Mountains which is called the Hell-Fire Club was the site of the orgies; but historians now say there is no evidence. I incline still to the legend on the general ground that what goes on in cities is nothing to do with what goes on in the country.

THE CLONLIFFE HAUNTINGS

One evening in the spring of 2008, I was taking a taxi from the city centre to Tolka Road, off Clonliffe Road, where I wrote most of this book. As the car crossed O'Connell Bridge, heading north, the driver suddenly started telling me a ghost story. I'd been in the taxi maybe two minutes and I certainly had not mentioned that I was writing *Haunted Dublin*.

The driver – we'll call him Paul – told me of a night when he drove a young woman home to her house in Clonliffe Road. She and her husband had just bought their dream home and were settling into domestic bliss. Paul told her that he'd grown up in the area, and knowing more or less where her house was, told her about strange events on that part of the street in the 1960s. He remembered 'the priest being called' to a house on Clonliffe Road, and his arrival by Ford Prefect. The kids, of which Paul was one, were hanging around the front of this house, but were chased away by adults as the priest entered. He's not quite sure what happened inside the house. He remembers an intimation of the unspeakable and he was left with the impression that maybe a possession and exorcism had occured there. The event left a mark with the local children, and the place was remembered as a 'haunted house'.

As Paul drew up alongside the curb in Clonliffe Road, his passenger asked him to point out the haunted house. When he did so, she said 'that's my house, I just knew it would be when you told me the story'. She and her husband had no odd experiences up this point, she said, and bade him goodnight. When Paul passed the house some weeks later, a 'For Sale' sign was up outside.

On my own journey home, Paul pointed out Clonliffe's haunted house. I won't include the address here, for the sake of the current resident's piece of mind and privacy. But I will say that there are far more haunted-looking residences on Clonliffe Road, with overgrown gardens or boarded-up windows. The 'haunted house' looks pretty welcoming in comparison.

After the taxi drew up outside my house, Paul and I spent the best part of an hour talking – or rather he talked and I took notes. Paul, as I said, had grown up on Tolka Road. He told me that the narrow strip between Clonliffe Road and the Tolka River – now containing Tolka Road and Clonliffe Gardens – was once an orchard, owned by a man called Tip Donnelly, who kept a herd of goats on his land. Weston St John Joyce, in his 1912 *The Neighbourhood of Dublin* makes reference to the area being called 'Donnelly's Orchard' as far back as the eighteenth century.

However, what had been once been Donnelly's land was bought up by Dublin City Council in the early twentieth century for the construction of housing – it was referred to as 'Donnelly's Orchard' in a Dáil Éireann discussion from 11 October 1933, on the future movement of city dwellers from one-room tenements to new houses in the suburbs.

'The white dog of Clonliffe Road' – this Dublin suburb doesn't seem scary at all. However, it's the site of a haunted house, as pointed out to me by taxi driver 'Paul'.

Even James Joyce's *Finnegans Wake* gives Donnelly mention, 'Such precedent is largely a cause to lack of collective continencies among Donnelly's orchard as lifelong the shadyside to Fairbrother's field.' Fairbrother's was another site designated for modern housing in the 1930s.

Donnelly does not seem to have been impressed with houses being built on his land, his being dead notwithstanding. In the 1960s, even when the area was nothing but houses, gardens and streets, Donnelly's herding stick could be heard by people walking home at night, with a tip-tapping on the ground as Tip Donnelly's ghost paced the streets, searching for his long-lost goats amongst long-gone apple trees.

Paul's father, who had also grown up on Tolka Road, had an unnerving experience as a child. He, his brothers and sisters woke up to find an apparition of a goat standing in their bedroom. Understandably, they fled downstairs, screaming. Their father – Paul's grandfather – was completely unimpressed, and 'leathered' them back up the stairs. They found the bedroom window open, the curtains billowing in the wind. This wasn't the only appearance of one of Tip Donnelly's goats; Paul's uncle later admitted

Tolka Road, off Clonliffe Road where Haunted Dublin *was written, and home to Tip Donnelly's ghost and spectral goats. It's also very close to Buck Jones's Red House.*

seeing it, and there were other reports from the neighbourhood.

To date, I've not seen any wayward goats or ghostly shepherds on Tolka Road.

Paul also told me other experiences he'd had, from the Southside of the city. In 1973, he worked in Tallaght. His 'missus' worked in Thomas Street in the city centre. They lived in an upstairs flat in Beechfield, Walkinstown. Another couple whom they became friends with lived downstairs, and they often had each other over for dinner or drinks.

Without warning, the couple downstairs moved out. Paul's wife caught the last glimpse of them jumping into a van full of belongings and driving away, without a goodbye. They just vanished. Other couples moved in and rapidly moved back out again. Paul and his wife were a little hurt and annoyed by how their apparent friends had treated them, but also thought the high turnover of new residents was a bit odd.

One night, Paul came in from a late shift. He wife would wait up for him on these occasions, but as she had an early start, after a while would say goodnight and head for bed. Paul read the paper, had a cigarette and soon followed her. As he was about to turn out the bedside light, he noticed a 'thing, like an indistinct cloud', which 'came out of the wall' and drifted over him. Paul was paralysed with fear, unable to even speak.

The 'thing' then vanished. He got up and, as he said, 'got rational'. He searched the house for intruders, checked doors and windows, but no one was there. He didn't sleep until first light.

Two weeks later, Paul came home early in the morning, having worked the all-night shift. As he approached the house, he noticed that the bedroom lights were off. Usually, his wife would be up by now, getting ready for work. He wondered if she had overslept. Inside the flat he found her, curled up in a blanket and sitting against a wall, sobbing. She had seen the same 'cloud thing' that Paul had seen.

They moved out of the flat that day.

Years later Paul dropped off a taxi customer in the same area, who knew the house. Some people had later bought it as a family home, and, he was told, kept the place in great shape, with a fine garden. Paul considered approaching the owners, and telling them his story. He never did.

He was in the area some years later, and decided to stop and park outside. He didn't recognise the house at first, then realised that it had been renumbered, because of new building developments, and its garage had been converted into a room. Sitting in his car, he looked up at his old bedroom window. The familiar sensation swept over him, and he left.

Paul told me one final story about a young auctioneer who he picked up one night, also on his way to Walkinstown. The passenger 'had a few drinks on him', and seemed to be reluctant to return home.

'Problems with the missus?'

'No, no I live with my parents.'

The young man started talking. It turned out that he'd had a weird experience while returning to the house a few nights before. As he approached the front door, he noticed a 'thing with red eyes staring at him from the roof'. This night, he was so afraid of going home that he'd gotten himself well-oiled to deal with it.

As they arrived at the house, the auctioneer stepped out of the car, and approached the house warily. Paul stayed in the car, and kept the engine running. The man reached the house safely, and went inside. Paul turned the car, and left, probably hoping that the red-eyed creature wasn't waiting inside.

DUBLIN'S HEADLESS HORSES, HORSEMEN ... AND BODILESS HEADS

Back in the Clonliffe Road neighbourhood, there is the tale of a headless horseman, riding a white horse, up Jones's Road and Russell Street, beside Croke Park. It's said to be one Buck Jones, who lived in a Georgian mansion known as the Red House, or Clonliffe House, about 200m from where I write these words.

Jones, by all accounts, was a handsome and refined eighteenth-century Dublin City Sheriff and notorious gambler. Interestingly, at some point, just prior to 1798, he became the owner of the Fishamble Street Theatre, which has a ghost story of its own (see later in this book). The Red House is now used by Crosscare, the social care agency of the Dublin Catholic Diocese, and has been incorporated into the grounds of Holy Cross College, Clonliffe Road.

Jones's Road is named after the Buck himself – it started life as a pathway he created as a short cut from North Circular Road to Clonliffe Road, sparing him a roundabout journey via Drumcondra. One might think that combining the twin careers of sheriff and gambler might cause a little conflict in a man's life – and you'd be right. That said, he was known to have shown great courage, nearly getting killed during escapades to arrest Larry Clinch, a desperado who attacked and burned the Belfast mail coach at Santry. Clinch and his gang actually held Jones under siege in his own home, before attacking on 6 November 1806. Jones had brought help, from members of the Tipperary Militia and a Captain O'Reilly. As the criminals broke into the house, a fracas broke out, with the soldiers wounding their own officer. Two of the attackers were killed, and the rest rounded up and jailed.

Unfortunately, Jones eventually favoured gambling over the upholding of the law and landed himself in debtor's prison. According to some versions of his story, he died while in detention, and was buried at a long-vanished unconsecrated cemetery in Ballybough, where he would have kept company with suicide victims, murderers and thieves – including the two killed in his own home. According to Weston St John Joyce, those deceased apparently had a stake driven through their chests, to stop these unhappy souls from wandering the roads at night and scaring the devil out the locals. Joyce contradicts the story about Jones's end, saying that after he *left* debtor's prison at Marshalsea Barracks, he lived in a small cabin near Mountjoy prison, where he 'was kept in the necessaries of life by a few faithful friends, who had known him in his better days, and who endeavoured to alleviate the old man's sorrow in his later years'.

Jones died in 1834, a 'ruined man'. St John Joyce goes on to say that 'there are not wanting some

The Red House, a Georgian mansion in the grounds of Clonliffe College. Once home to Buck Jones, who now haunts the street named after him – Jones Road, next to Croke Park.

who aver that they have seen him, at dead of night, a tall stately figure on horseback, noiselessly riding about the neighbourhood of Jones's Road'.

Ballybough's 'Mud Island' harboured a leper colony, and dozens of criminals, who used it as a launch pad for their forays up Summerhill and into the city. A gibbet was once situated there, and was used to despatch highwaymen and thieves before staking them and consigning them to the earth. While there's no talk of vampires with these stories, it's worth bearing in mind that Ballybough is about ten minutes' walk from the childhood home of Bram Stoker (1847-1912), author of *Dracula*. I'm sure Bram would have been impressed by these tales, especially as his mother had a morbid tendency to fill her sickly son's head with dark tales.

SPOOK COACHES

Dublin city and outskirts seem to be beset by several other ghostly coaches and horsemen, who seem to give scant regard for twenty-first-century traffic problems.

In the Liberties, a headless horseman was said to ride, once the dark evenings set in, around the Blackpitts area. This story is connected to some macabre family goings-on in the Roper family. Thomas Roper, First Viscount Baltinglass, lived at Roper's Rest, and died there in around 18 February

1637, and the story that comes from around this time concerns the death of a family member, whose corpse was left for an unprecedented amount of time before being buried.

In Tallaght, a coach drawn by six headless horses and driven by a headless coachman was seen belting around the back roads near the mountains. Curiously, this story never seems to have been associated with the Hellfire Club; instead, the coach is said to have contained an Archdeacon Bulkeley, who lived in Oldbawn House in the seventeenth century.

Meanwhile, across west Dublin, in the parish of Clondalkin, golfers at Newlands Golf Club in the 1920s reported seeing a phantom coach that would arrive down the lonely avenue on dark nights. This was supposed to contain the wraith of Arthur Wolfe, later Baron Kilwarden and Chief Justice of Ireland, who was piked to death in his carriage during an insurrection led by Robert Emmet in 1803.

The famous barrister, MP and commentator Jonah Barrington wrote:

The moment the cry went forth, the carriage was stopped, and the door torn open. The clergyman and Miss Wolfe got out and ran; the latter was suffered to escape; but the pikemen pursued, and having come up with Mr Wolfe, mangled and murdered in a horrid manner as fine and inoffensive a young gentleman as I ever knew.

Hundreds of the murderers now surrounded the carriage, ambitious only who should first spill the blood of a chief justice; a multitude of pikemen at once assailed him, but his wounds proved that he had made many efforts to evade them. His hands were lacerated all over in the act of resistance; but after a long interval of torture, near thirty stabs in various parts of his body incapacitated him from struggling further with his destiny. They dragged him into the street; yet, when conveyed into a house, he was still sensible, and able to speak a few words, but soon after expired, to the great regret of all those who knew him well, as I did, and were able to separate his frivolity from his excellent qualities.

THE BODILESS HEAD

On Harmonstown Road in Artane, there was a haunting by a head – but no body! Sean Carroll told me of being a child in bed in around 1960; he remembers getting up and looking out the window with brothers, where 'all of the neighbourhood men were searching the gardens for a head'. Someone had apparently witnessed a disembodied head moving up the street. The ghost-hunting vigilantes were carrying everything from shovels and rakes to carving knives and hurleys. 'I didn't sleep for weeks,' he said, 'I was more afraid of them than the head.'

PORTOBELLO HARBOUR, RATHMINES BRIDGE, DUBLIN

While not strictly a ghost-horse story, it does involve horses. At 9p.m. on Saturday 6 April 1861, a horse-drawn bus, driven by a Patrick Hardy had just deposited a passenger at the bridge at Portobello, when one of his horses reared up.

A bright light seemed to be rising from the Grand Canal water and turning into a human shape. Both of the bus's horses became frightened, knocking the bus through the bridge railings into the canal. Six passengers were drowned. The conductor managed to escape, while the driver was rescued by a passing policeman. They blamed the ghost of a lock-keeper, who had drowned himself after being sacked for drunkenness.

La Touche Bridge, also known as Portobello Bridge, near Rathmines … where victims were 'blinded by a bright light that rose from the canal'.

Interestingly, three years earlier, on a November evening, a soldier based at nearby Portobello Barracks was walking along the canal to meet his girlfriend. He and two passers by were blinded by a bright light that rose from the canal. The soldier fell into the canal and drowned. The two other people swore that the light had risen from the water before taking a human shape.

THE TODAY FM HAUNTINGS ON ABBEY STREET

Irish commercial radio station Today FM moved office in the spring of 2008, from their converted Georgian house in Abbey Street, to Digges Lane. Before they left, however, Bernie Jameson, a Today FM newsreader, joined other members of staff in publicly declaring the radio station was haunted, on the Ray D'Arcy show in February 2008.

A few months later I had a conversation with Bernie, in which she summarised her experiences. She worked the late shift in the newsroom, until midnight. While at her desk, she became convinced

The haunted newsroom: Today FM's former headquarters, at 123 and 124 Upper Abbey Street.

that she could hear a woman's voice quietly singing a lullaby in the corner of the room. If she walked towards it, slowly, the singing would stop. If she went back to her desk, the singing would restart. At first she thought that it was a radio turned on low, but as time went on, she realised that it had to be something else. Other staff, around eight people in total, started mentioning strange phenomena – studio chairs spinning by themselves, or apparitions walking through walls.

The walls in question were new structures, put in place when the building was refurbished as a radio station. In the past, the house had been integrated with Jervis Street Hospital, now the location of the Jervis Street Shopping Centre. The feeling at Today FM was that if there were ghosts of nurses pacing the rooms, then they would ignore the new walls, and follow their old paths.

When Bernie told this story, security staff from the entire block, including Marks & Spencers, contacted the radio station to pass on their own experiences. These included seeing nurses in outdated uniforms in the elevators and corridors and one report of a nurse walking straight through a wall in the outside loading bay on Abbey Street.

While the publicity surely didn't do Today FM any harm, Bernie and the other staff seem to have genuinely experienced something odd. She assured me that so far, their new location doesn't seem to be haunted.

STRANGE HAPPENINGS ON BENBURB STREET

Dublin's Benburb Street passes through centuries of history, with Collins Barracks – the oldest continuously occupied in the world – now the National Museum on one side, and Croppies Acre, where bodies of 1798 rebels were thrown on the other. Along with the oldest barracks and soldiers, naturally came the oldest trade – street prostitutes could still be seen operating along Benburb Street until the advent of the Luas, Dublin's new tram system, which cuts along the street instead of cars. The street walkers have gone elsewhere in the neighbourhood and not without controversy either, as the residents will attest.

It was probably midnight on a Saturday, September or October 1993 – I can't remember exactly. I was living at the Phoenix Park end of North Circular Road, in a damp, three-room, one-window (facing north) basement flat. I made sure that all my post was addressed to 'Dave Walsh, Debasement'.

I had just arrived back with a bag of records and CDs after my weekly stint on a Dublin pirate radio station, before some friends arrived by car to take me to a party. It was not a long journey – just down Infirmary Road to Parkgate Street and onto Benburb Street.

The party was in an old ramshackle three-story redbrick house, about fifty metres from the gate of Collins Barracks. The tenants were throwing a hooley to celebrate the end of an era – they were moving out of the house, as it was destined for demolition. In the main ground-floor room, the air was thick with dry ice, and the floor crammed with people dancing to the DJ's tunes. The dry ice rose in a column through the stairwell – faces loomed out of the fog as partygoers ascended and descended. Another DJ was playing in a packed first-floor room – but the visibility was slightly better. On the top floor was, oddly enough, a kitchen and living room. There wasn't much space here either.

A couple of my friends decided to roll up a joint; but there was no space whatsoever. We walked back across the landing, into a dark, empty room. I flicked the switch; nothing, the light didn't work. I poked around in the room until my eyes adjusted. There were two single beds and a fireplace, set into a diagonal in the corner. The window, facing the back of the house, was open. On one of the beds lay a young man, face down dressed in a denim jacket and jeans, completely out for the count. I found a candle in an ancient brass candlestick, encrusted with years of wax, and lit it.

The sleeper never stirred. My colleagues sat on the other bed, and went about their task. I was supposed to provide them with light, but kept wandering off to explore the shadows, taking the light

Derelict house on Benburb Street, next to where the author experienced strange happenings.

with me, which drew complaints from the others. I found some burns on the wallpaper above the mantelpiece – the result of letting the candle sit too close to the wall. They looked like figures in some sort of cave painting. I turned around to face the room, and suddenly felt unsettled.

I walked back to the bed.

'I don't like it in here', I announced.

'Dave doesn't like it in here.' I had voiced the discomforts the others had been keeping to themselves. They looked at each other, and then fled the room, leaving me on my own. I was down the stairs behind them like a shot.

We didn't leave the party, so maybe we weren't that scared … or perhaps we had just scared each other. Maybe the indignity of fleeing the party was a worse prospect than encountering what may or may not have been in the room. Perhaps it was the mind's way of glossing over the completely bizarre and explicable. We had a drink, danced and mingled.

Sometime later, I climbed the stairs again, still with the lighted candle before me. Outside 'The Room', I met two girls who looked at me in a concerned fashion. I recognised one of them; she was a friend of a friend's sister.

'Have you been in that room?' one of them asked.

'Yes … why?'

'You do know it's haunted, don't you?'

'Well, I did think it was a bit weird in there.'

She went to on tell me of her experiences. She used to live in the house, in the room downstairs, and there regular occurrences of strange noises from the room. One night, when she knew she was alone in the house, the noises started. Heavy footsteps could be heard in the room above, and shifting of furniture. She called out, but no one answered. She didn't dare go look.

Then noise started downstairs. She yelled again, and this time a voice answered back. She felt relieved. Personally, I might have found the prospect of someone shouting back at me a little *more* alarming at the time. It was, fortunately, one of her housemates. They joined forces and raced to the top floor to investigate – but the room above was calm, quiet, and undisturbed. There was no sign of life – but then, perhaps life isn't what they should have been looking for.

I still think of that night, whenever I pass along Benburb Street. The old house is long gone, replaced by a complex of new, modern apartments. I wonder if any of the residents, living on or around the third floor, ever experience any strange sounds or sensations?

When digging around for any older stories that might be connected to Benburb Street, I came across mentions of a ghost in Collins Barracks, now the Decorative Arts and History branch of the National Museum. Staff, I'm told, maintain that the third floor harbours the ghost of a soldier who killed himself. I also came across some strange stories from nearby Hendrick Street, in John

Derelict shops, Benburb Street.

J. Dunne's 1977 book, *Haunted Ireland*.

Almost no one knows where Hendrick Street is anymore; it's a street parallel to Benburb Street, off Queen Street near Blackhall Place. Practically nothing is left of the original tall Georgian buildings that once stood there, with their gable ends facing the street, like Dutch townhouses. After many years of grandeur, the houses slid into disrepair, and were broken up into slum tenements before final demolition.

According to Dunne, in 1914, the Brophy family lived in flats in one of the houses; number 7. The house had been inhabited by a Mr Watt who seems to have left something behind him … such as his ghost.

Throughout their residency, the Brophys would regularly wake up in the middle of the night to the sound of bare feet slapping on the floorboards, always starting at the top of the house, and coming quickly downstairs to the front hall. The sound would stop, and then start again fifteen minutes later at the top of the house – but never could be heard going *upstairs* again.

One of the last remaining old buildings on Hendrick Street, close to the notoriously haunted number 7.

Somehow, the Brophys stuck this out – I'm not sure I understand how or why – all through the 1920 and on to the 1950s. The other residents would also report sounds emanating from the top floor flat, which was permanently locked and unoccupied.

George Brophy, who lived in the house until 1963, told Dunne the unnerving story of having returned to the house at 1.30a.m., having been out visiting friends. He entered the house, with his bicycle on his shoulder, and proceeded to carry it up to his flat.

He was about to unlock his door when the sound of bare feet began, somewhere above him. He knew that within seconds, the footsteps would descend the stairs and cross the landing where he stood. Panicked, he tried to open his flat door, but fumbled with the keys. Sweat broke out on his brow, as the footsteps grew closer.

Suddenly, the footsteps reached the landing and Brophy felt what he described to Dunne as 'a gush of cold air' whipping across the landing behind him, as whatever it was descended to the floor below.

Brophy also recounted a 'poltergeist manifestation'. Apparently something of a night owl, he was sitting alone in the flat at 12.50a.m., when he decided to eat something before heading to bed. As he walked towards the dresser, a steel-handled knife rose from it, and was flung 'four or five feet into the air' above his head, before falling back to its home on top of the dresser.

Brophy seems to have been the more courageous of the residents, in that he was willing to engage at some level with the haunting, while other number 7 Hendrick Street dwellers barely ever left their rooms after dark, if it could be avoided.

MORE DUBLIN POLTERGEISTS

'Ghosts Want To Kill My Kids' ran the front page headline in the *Irish Daily Mirror* on 27 August 2007; 'Mum's terror in haunted house'. According to a rather breathless Maeve Quigley writing for the paper, thirty-seven-year-old Martha Cousins, mother of three, said that she was 'being forced to flee her house of horrors because evil spirits want to kill her family'.

Cousins also claimed that ghosts had caused the fire brigade to be called after a fire broke out in the attic of her three-bedroom house in the Ballycragh estate in Tallaght, Co. Dublin, in an 'attempt to harm her three children', seventeen-year-old Gemma, thirteen-year-old Daniel and seven-year-old Saoirse. There were also reports of 'footsteps, banging and doors slamming', which in itself doesn't sound odd for a house full of kids. However, Martha claims that Saoirse has been 'kicked by one the spirits, and I have been punched and bitten':

> Ever since I moved into this house 12 years ago, there have been incidents of hauntings. At first there were only little things happening – like a pen or something flying across the room. I used to tell my kids that it was just their dad playing tricks on them.
>
> But things have steadily got worse since my husband Stephen died six years ago in a car crash. The ghosts thrive on tragedy, and have steadily got worse. It is at the point where I cannot live there any more as I am fearful for the safety of my children. These ghosts thrive on tragedy, and they have got steadily worse.

Martha also claimed that 'the noise is terrible and they also do things like turn the heating and cooker on and off and leave the fridge door open. I had someone checking the house when I was on holidays and she said she heard doors banging and her dog began to whimper because it could sense something. The rooms upstairs are really cold, no matter if the heating is on or not.'

She said that her youngest child was too afraid to go upstairs; her son won't sleep in his room, so they all ended up sleeping in the living room, where the door keeps mysteriously opening.

Then the story starts skating off track – Martha, it seems, has engaged a 'medium' to cleanse the house every day: this person has told her that the problems will *not* go away as the house is built on 'ley lines' that 'lead to the sinister Hellfire Club, built on a burial ground and home to eighteenth-century satanists'.

Dublin Castle, where Garda Sergeant Lowe's reportedly had his poltergeist experiences.

Now if it's one subject that gets fortean researchers, antiquarians and archaeologists spitting bile, it is ley lines, as no one can actually agree as to what they are, or if they even exist.

Proposed in 1921 by British amateur archaeologist Alfred Watkins (1855-1935), ley lines are nothing more than the hypothetical alignment of sites of geographical or archaeological interest, like megaliths or other ancient monuments. Sometimes these alignments are joined by ancient pathways, thought to be used for ceremonial purposes, like the Nazca lines in Peru. Others in ancient European culture are less spectacular; to claim that there's a straight line between monument A and monument B is hardly mindblowing stuff – any two dots can make a straight line, and can signify a pathway or road, defensive structures, property markings, or simply some neat surveying by ambitious stone-age humans.

However, Watkins's ley lines, already controversial within archaeological fields, were later hijacked by the new-age community. As a result, it's now widely believed that ley lines are conduits of some kind of vague 'energy', and that they attract ghosts, UFOs, Bigfoot, poltergeists, even the Knights Templar and the Holy Grail.

The arguments for and against ley lines and their meaning, are far too complicated to go into here – but I have my doubts about a ley line connecting Martha Cousins's house and the Hellfire Club.

According to the *Irish Daily Mirror*, the medium has been clearing spirits every day – but as soon as she 'gets rid of some, another vortex opens and seven or eight more ghosts come through'. Martha had apparently been begging Dublin City Council for a new home, but the requests had 'fallen on deaf ears', even after she had posted a DVD to them, presumably containing evidence of the haunting.

The Olympia Theatre's stage door – the theatre was reported to be home to a strange presence.

DUBLIN CASTLE POLTERGEIST

A rather odd article appeared in the *Garda Review* in 1955. A Sergeant Lowe wrote about his being stationed in Dublin Castle when he was still a raw young recruit. He reported being alone in the dormitory, shared with thirteen other young men, when the light would switch off by itself. He would switch it on again and see he was still alone. Then he heard the sound of coal being shovelled in the kitchen. He snuck down the hallway to the kitchen door. The sound ceased as he opened it, and he saw that no coal had been put on the fire, and the coal shovel was as he had left it. A friend of mine who works in Dublin Castle told me that Castle staff maintain that one of the buildings in the Upper Castle Yard is haunted by the ghost of a woman, said to be pining away for a love who never returned from battle.

THEATRICAL POLTERGEISTS

The Olympia Theatre on Dame Street was subject to a series of noises and knockings in the 1960s. Austrian paranormal researcher Hans Holzer (*b.*1920), along with British psychic Sybil Leek (1917-1982), visited the theatre in 1965, to interview the staff and explore the building.

Staff had reported banging, rattling of windows, phantom footsteps and the sense of a 'presence' pervading the building, which has been rebuilt once and refurbished once since it first opened in 1879. One of the dressing rooms, number 9, had the door knocked on several times – and no one was

The Olympia Theatre, Dame Street,
said to be haunted by the ghost
of an innocent man killed
during the 1916 Rising.

outside. One season, during a pantomime, an entire dressing room was ransacked – apparently by a poltergeist, according to a former stage manager.

The same stage manager, Jeremy Swan, told Holzer that he had walked out of a washroom one night to see a small yellow light, or as he put it, a 'glow' moving along the corridor at knee height, towards dressing room 9. As he followed it, a door slammed in his face.

Another man, Tom Connor, the electrician, said that the rostrum he had been sitting on suddenly rose up with him on it, although he was alone at the time.

Holzer then quizzed his psychic sidekick – who had not been listening to the interviews. She reckoned that there was the 'impression' of a young man who wanted to escape the theatre and the some violence was involved, not involving the Olympia. According to stagehand Alfred Barden, a civilian had been shot in the theatre by mistake during the 1916 Rising, after being chased in there. Holzer and Leek reckoned that the ghost was of this young man, stressfully retracing his last footsteps around the theatre before his killers caught up with him …

Plaque on Fishamble Street, commemorating the first performance of Handel's Messiah *at the music hall – site of some later hauntings.*

KNOCKING AT MR NEAL'S

Mr Neale's Music Hall, or the Fishamble Street Theatre as it later became known, is long gone. But it was a famous place in its day. In April 1742, a year after it opened, it was the venue for the first performance of Handel's *Messiah* for charity, to raise money for Mercer's Hospital. It was later owned by the infamous Buck Jones, who now gallops, headless, around the streets near Croke Park.

In the mid-nineteenth century, John Hogan, a builder's apprentice, was doing repairs to the theatre, and slept-over every night in the Green Room. Every night, knockings would start at 10p.m., and continue for fifteen minutes. His request to sleep in a different room was turned down, so he spent each night pulling the blankets over his head. Apparently the knocking continued for another sixty years, until the theatre was demolished.

SOME WILL NEVER SETTLE DOWN

Dermot McManus's *The Middle Kingdom* includes a story about a poltergeist in some unspecified part of Dublin's outskirts, around 1935. A Mrs Dean was the caretaker of a cemetery, and also had to take care of her invalid husband and her dying mother. One cold, moonlit January night, a Dr Sellars and a nurse visited to check on the mother. When Mrs Dean's own well-being was inquired into, she said she was having some trouble with the 'crowd out there', indicating the cemetery.

'I wouldn't mind it their being a bit fractious at first, but some will never settle down.' She mentioned being happy that a well-known, influential and recently-deceased person was safely buried

Fishamble Street, site of the famous music hall, now replaced by a later residential and office building.

in a strong vault, 'or he'd be worse than any of them with their antics'.

Although Mrs Dean was known for her frankness, this left Sellars somewhat bemused. He communicated his scepticism to Mrs Dean, and made to leave with the nurse. As he approached the door, there was a massive bang on it, and it started shaking violently. Sellars put his hand on the door, swung it open – but it was a calm January night outside.

'Didn't I tell you, now, doctor? Sure that's what they do be annoying me with all the time.'

As I was going up the stairs, I met a man who wasn't there ...

Terry Ward wrote to me, while I was compiling *Haunted Dublin*, to tell me a story that had been in his family for decades, concerning an experience his grandfather John Dunne had on Dublin's Inns Quay.

In the early twentieth century, Dunne's siblings lived in various different tenements along the quays. Dunne, however, joined the British army in 1913, fought in the Great War, and when he returned home, joined the Irish army.

Extensive damage to the family home on Merchants Quay during the War of Independence prompted a move to 7 Inns Quay, near the Four Courts. Somehow, the Civil War devastation wreaked upon the court buildings in 1922 didn't cause any damage to their new home. This is surprising, as I've seen photographs taken during the shelling of the Four Courts, with houses on Inns Quay reduced to rubble.

The Inns Quay house was a five-story tenement building, with a dark staircase. A similar house has recently been restored at 15 Usher's Island, thanks to its inclusion in James Joyce's story *The Dead*.

Later on, in the 1930s or 40s, Dunne was visiting his sisters at 7 Inns Quay. As he was climbing the dimly lit stairs towards their room, he met a man on the stairs. Dunne beckoned him to come down, and made way for him, as the stairs were narrow. The man did not appear to acknowledge Dunne, but started descending the stairs. As he neared Dunne, the man started fading away, and then vanished entirely.

'My grandfather was shocked by the experience, and the story lives on in the family to this day.'

The Four Courts on Inns Quay, near where John Dunne met 'the man who wasn't there'.

BLACK DOGS

According to writer John J. Dunne (a different John Dunne to the Inns Quay one), in the late 1930s, a 'long correspondence' filled the letters page of the *Dublin Evening Mail*, featuring all sorts of legends and traditions from the Templeogue area of Dublin, including a place with the intriguing name of 'Pussy's Leap'. In a letter written by someone who signed themselves 'Black Cat', a story was recounted about a *black dog* that haunted Pussy's Leap. And Templeogue isn't a million miles away from Killakee, which was haunted by a giant black cat in the 1960s. Confused yet?

Black Cat wrote:

> As an old resident and one who spent my childhood in the district, I would like to relate an experience of 40 years ago [presumably the 1890s] at Pussy's Leap. At that time there was only delivery of letters in the morning, and if you required the night letters you had to call to the post office in Templeogue.
>
> It was a moonlit winter evening, about 9p.m., and I was walking home with the letters, accompanied by a servant maid from Cherryfield. As my companion and I approached Pussy's Leap, a black dog crossed our path. It got larger as it ran across, and gradually went out of sight, with the sound of chains.
>
> I need not state here my fears, but I managed to get home without losing consciousness. For years after, I was always afraid to pass the 'leap' at night. Strange, the servant maid did not see the dog, but heard the rattling chains.

Nearby Rathfarnham Castle is also reputed to have a phantom dog; maybe it's the same phantom animal! The story is set in the 1840s, when a pond in the castle grounds had frozen over in the midst of a severe winter. A group of skaters would use the pond for some fun; we never seem to get winters like that in Ireland anymore. In the story, tragedy struck when a man fell through the ice. People watched as the man's dog went to the rescue, diving into the hole to rescue his master. Alas, both the skater and the poor old dog were drowned. A monument was later erected to the courageous animal's memory, and for years afterwards, the dog would be seen near the pond, and in other areas of the castle grounds.

THE BLACK DOG OF CABRA

Meanwhile, on the other side of the city in Cabra, another semi-rural area that has since been overrun by 1930s and later housing developments, another black dog was reported.

Statue of John McNeill Boyd, which is said to be haunted by the ghost of his loyal dog.

There was an old house there, long since vanished, and replaced by semi-detached houses. A John Toler lived there, the first Earl of Norbury. Norbury was infamous as Dublin's 'Hanging Judge' – and the man who tried Robert Emmet and others implicated in the 1803 rebellion. And apparently Norbury was not a popular figure in Cabra, either – he was a feared and hated man.

Norbury eventually died, but his legacy of fear resonanted throughout the nineteenth century, through the appearances of a massive phantom black dog, reported to have been seen skulking around Cabra's lanes – and in particular around Norbury's former home. The people of Cabra believed that the dog was a manifestation of Norbury's ghost, come back to haunt them – or perhaps he couldn't go away. There's a story that Norbury had a young Blanchardstown man hung for sheep stealing; his widow died from grief not long after. On her deathbed, she rather predictably cursed Norbury, ensuring that he would never get a decent night's sleep again. Norbury is said to have suffered from chronic insomnia in his later years.

Whether Norbury was haunting the people of Cabra, or was simply stuck in an endless cycle of sleeplessness, the local people had to cope with the prospect of walking the roads of Cabra at night, constantly primed for the padding of big paws, or panting from a massive mouthful of teeth, while a broken chain dragged along behind the phantom hound.

JOHN McNEILL BOYD'S DOG

A less frightening dog, specifically a Newfoundland, haunts the grave in the grounds of St Patrick's Cathedral of John McNeill Boyd (1812-1861), captain of the HMS *Ajax*, who was lost at sea on 9 February 1861. After Boyd drowned, the dog refused to leave his master's grave and slowly starved

The tomb of John McNeill Boyd,
reportedly haunted by his loyal dog.

to death. The loyal hound has also been seen, according to former Dean David Wilson, inside the cathedral beside an impressive statute of Boyd.

However, some confused versions of this story claim that Boyd is buried in Glasnevin Cemetery. Several incarnations of the story appear both on the internet and in print, most recently in the *Dublin People*, 3 July 2008, which states that a ghostly dog has been recently seen in Glasnevin Cemetery. The article, which is in itself confusing, says that a 'paranormal investigator', Tallaght man Martin Black, has established that 'the animal is known to be a demon dog that belonged to a historian who died in the 1700s'. The unnamed journalist suggests that the dog is that of John McNeill Boyd, and references a website called paranormaldatabase.com for this information.

The thing is, John McNeill Boyd *most definitely* isn't buried in Glasnevin Cemetery, which is for Catholics. He was of the Church of Ireland faith, and is *most definitely* interred at St Patrick's Cathedral, Dublin. I have, in fact, visited and photographed his tombstone.

According to *The Times* newspaper of 12 February 1861, Boyd was swept out to sea, along with

The tomb of John McNeill Boyd, most definitely in the grounds of St Patrick's Cathedral..

some fourteen of his crew, while standing on the eastern pier at Dún Laoghaire. They were trying to rescue the crew of a brig, *Neptune*, which had gone adrift during an appalling storm. There's a huge monument to this event on Dún Laoghaire pier. According to the myths surrounding Boyd, his unnamed Newfoundland dog was in the rescue boat that went looking for survivors.

While his crewmen were washed ashore some days later, and buried at Carrickbrennan, near Dún Laoghaire, Boyd's body wasn't found for weeks, and the grave dug for him was never used. He was instead brought to St Patrick's, and the ghost story tells us that the dog walked beside the coffin all the way there (or to the unlikely venue of Glasnevin, in some versions), before lying on the filled-in grave and eventually starving to death. Apparently Dean Wilson, who died in 1950, was one of those who often saw the dog inside the cathedral, near Boyd's statue.

The Times, 12 and 13 of February 1861
Dublin People, 3 July 2008

THE GHOSTS OF
ARCHBISHOP MARSH,
SWIFT AND STELLA

Dublin's little-known Marsh's library is said to harbour a ghost. Nestled in behind St Patrick's Cathedral, just off Kevin Street, it has an entrance off St Patrick's Close, through a mysterious archway and up some fairytale steps.

Founded in 1701 by Archbishop Narcissus Marsh (1638-1713), it was the first public library in Ireland, and houses more than 25,000 books relating to the sixteenth, seventeenth and eighteenth centuries. These, according to its website, cover 'medicine, law, science, travel, navigation, mathematics, music, surveying and classical literature'. It's certainly worth a visit; the interior has splendid dark oak carved and lettered bookcases, and more interestingly, three wired 'cages' where the readers used to be locked in with rare books.

In the three centuries since Marsh's death, a ghost has been sometimes reported from the library, drifting around and searching through books. There's a story attached to this: Marsh was the guardian of Grace Marsh, his nineteen-year-old niece. She also acted as his housekeeper. Bored with the scholarly, ecclesiastical life, she fell in love with a salty sea captain. Marsh disapproved, and tried to intervene, but the couple eloped, never to be seen again.

Marsh wrote in his diary:

> This evening betwixt eight and nine o'clock my niece Grace Marsh (not having the fear of God before her eyes) stole privately out of my house … and (as it reported) was that night married to Chas Proby Vicar of Castleknock in a tavern and was bedded there with him – Lord consider my affliction.

Grace, in what could have been either a fit of cruelty or conscience, left a note for Marsh inside one of the library books, supposedly asking for forgiveness.

Archbishop Marsh never did track down the note, and so never learned his beloved relative's last

Marsh's Library, Dublin's 300-year-old public library, is still home to the wandering wraith of Archbishop Narcissus Marsh, who searches the books for a lost letter from his errant niece.

words to him. Now he seems to be stuck in an infinite cycle, searching every book …

Some of the stories surrounding this haunting claim that the library ghost is that of Charles Maturin (1782-1924), author of *Melmoth the Wanderer*, who spent many hours (alive) in the library, researching and writing. Maturin had some eccentric habits, such as sticking a communion host to his forehead as a sign that he wasn't to be disturbed. The ghost has also been connected to Jonathan Swift (1667-1745), Dean of St Patrick's Cathedral and author of *Gulliver's Travels*, perhaps having popped into the library from St Patrick's next door. The Dean's ghost seems to appear all over the place – elsewhere in Ireland in some cases – along with that of his beloved Stella.

Some years ago, probably in about 1995, I heard a story from a staff member of what was then the Meath Hospital, at the corner of Heytesbury Street and Long Lane. Having been established in 1753, the hospital moved to this location in 1822, and then in 1998 relocated to Tallaght. I was told that ghosts had been seen in the hospital – often the figure of a woman drifting towards a very old, locked door. The general feeling amongst staff was that it was Esther Johnson (1681-1728), known as Stella, the life-long love of Swift.

St Patrick's Cathedral – home to McNeill Boyd's ghost dog, and where Dean Jonathan Swift is buried.

He had tutored Stella when she was eight and he was in his twenties, but as adults they developed a relationship of sorts. However, during his time in London, he fell for a young girl who he called 'Vanessa'. She was Esther Vanhomrigh (1688-1723) – the other Esther. When he returned to Ireland, he at some point quietly married Stella, it seems. When Vanessa, who had moved to Ireland in pursuit of him, found this out, she raised hell by writing to Stella.

Stella, her heart broken that Swift was 'seeing someone else on the side' showed the letter to the Dean, who galloped out to Vanessa's house, gave her a withering glare, threw her letter on the table, and marched out. She died three weeks later – apparently of a broken heart. So did Stella, but five years later. Swift survived them both, but his body is interred in the same coffin as Stella's, within the floor of St Patrick's Cathedral.

At the time, I wondered what the ghost of Stella might be doing wandering the hallways of the Meath hospital. However, Dublin was a very different place in the early eighteenth century. Where the hospital was built was once the 'Dean's Vineyard', or the garden for the cathedral, and where Swift would have had a paddock for his horse. The wall separating the hospital from Long Lane

Plaque marking the burial site of Jonathan Swift and Esther Johnson, St Patrick's Cathedral – the Dean still haunts the Deanery across the street.

includes sections that Swift himself had built.

So, was it the ghost of Stella, or some unhappy victim of the health service?

THE DEANERY GHOST

Very Reverend Victor Griffin (*b.*1924), Dean of St Patrick's between 1969 and 1991, describes his encounters with Swift's ghost in his book *Mark of Protest*.

According to Dean Griffin, there's a tradition that Swift haunts the Deanery of St Patrick's, just across the St Patrick's Close from the cathedral. As soon as he and his wife, Daphne, had moved into the house in 1969, they were asked 'Did you see Swift's ghost?'

They had not, and made it known that they didn't believe in such things. However, over time, they both became aware of a 'benevolent presence' in the Deanery. Daphne, who was wheelchair bound, often spent time in the house on her own, but never found it an uncomfortable place. Sometimes, while in the kitchen, she would have the impression that someone was with her, 'gently keeping her company', by standing over her wheelchair. A couple of times she thought it was their sons, Kevin or Timothy, and turned to face them – but there would be no one there.

Dean Griffin wrote:

Although always sceptical about ghosts and preferring natural explanations to supernatural, I had nevertheless what might be described as a ghostly experience in the Deanery, when late one evening, in the dim light of the hall, I saw what appeared to be the figure of a man going up the stairs and disappearing into the large bedroom on the landing. I assumed it was my brother-in-law who was staying with us at the time, and had spent the evening out on the town with friends from his Trinity days. I called to say 'Goodnight', but there was no reply.

He remarked on this to his wife, who wondered if Brian was 'all right'. This prompted Dean Griffin to visit his brother-in-law's room – but there was no one there. Six months later, the exact same phenomenon was repeated, 'same figure, same hour, same room'.

The Dean became convinced that someone was hiding in the house, and undertook a thorough search. His wife, who was not in the least bit put out by the apparition, told him 'you'll find nobody. Don't worry – there's no intruder.'

It later occurred to Dean Griffin that the room was the same where Swift had spent his 'declining years', and wondered if the 'mysterious figure might have been the ghost of some old retainer seeing his comfortably settled for the night before he himself retired to bed'.

THE SHELBOURNE HOTEL GHOST

When Austrian paranormal investigator Hans Holzer visited Dublin back in 1965, he stayed in the Shelbourne Hotel, on the corner of Stephen's Green and Kildare Street. The five-star hotel was opened in 1824 by one Martin Burke, when he bought up a row of adjoining townhouses. Recently redeveloped, when Holzer would have visited, the floor and room structure would have been somewhat higgledy-piggledy, due to the differing designs of the original houses.

According to Holzer's rather florid *The Lively Ghosts of Ireland: True tales of the supernatural from the ancient seat of Ghost Lore* (1967), he had no prior knowledge of any ghost in the Shelbourne. The management assured him there were no strange reports, but when his psychic friend Sybil Leek arrived, she announced that her small room, room 526, was haunted. Coincidence, or what?

Leek reported that while lying in bed, sometime after 2.20a.m., she heard a noise from the bathroom that at first she thought was a cat – but then clearly heard a child crying. Leek spoke, asking, 'What's the matter?'

'I'm frightened', came the response.

Leek invited the child, or whatever it was, to the bed. She felt the bed being touched and the weight of a child helping itself onto the bed, before a child's arm was laid around her neck. Incredibly, she fell asleep but awoke at 6.30a.m. with a numb right arm.

The next night, she was awoken again, this time by the sound of 'material seemingly moving over the floor in the area of the bathroom'. She switched on the light and heard a noise by the window, which she found closed – despite her having left it open.

She sat down to take notes, but was immediately joined by a presence, 'It was a small girl, about seven years old' in a woolen nightshirt, who seemed extremely exhausted. Leek told the girl to go bed, which she did, climbing into the one bed in the room. Leek asked the child her name. 'Mary Masters' was the reply. After that, the conversation became vague and indistinct, though she seemed to be looking for someone called Sophia – so Leek again fell asleep with 'Mary' beside her.

The following night, Holzer and his wife Catherine joined Leek in her room, for a 'trance session'. This involved Leek going into a trance, to channel Mary Masters for the others, which she seemingly did. The conversation documented in Holzer's book is rather fragmented, but is mostly childish. Holzer actually described the child as appearing 'petulant' and weak; few of his questions were answered directly.

However, he endeavoured to 'to send her away' by telling her to 'go to sleep and dream of her mama'. She sobbed … but eventually drifted away. Leek came out of the trance, remembering nothing.

The Shelbourne Hotel, Stephen's Green, home of Mary Master's ghost.

Statue outside the Shelbourne Hotel, Stephen's Green, where Sybil Leek and Hans Holzer 'discovered' a ghost.

Despite Leek and Holzer's experiences, there do not seem be any prior documented reports of hauntings at the Shelbourne – and none since either. When I called the Shelbourne and spoke to the head of marketing, Aisling McDermott, she told me that while the hotel got regular requests from TV companies about filming the haunted room, the hotel staff and management knew very little of Holzer and Leek's story. She confirmed that to her knowledge there have been no reported hauntings *since* 1965 – or least none that she knew of. Room 526, where Leek had her experiences, no longer exists: the entire hotel was gutted and rebuilt from the inside, while retaining the original façade.

Perhaps Mary Masters was, like Holzer and Leek, just passing through.

ST STEPHEN'S GREEN

There are other ghosts and strange events reported from Stephen's Green. Iveagh House, once owned by the Guinness family, but now the Department of Foreign Affairs, used to draw crowds every Holy Thursday. The watchers hoped to see a sign of the cross appear on a pane of glass in one of the windows. The unlikely legend surrounding this phenomenon describes a servant girl that lay dying in her room – a Catholic in what would have been a Protestant household. She had been refused a priest by her employer, who on catching the girl with rosary beads, flung them out the window.

For the record, this legend may not be a reference to the Guinness family – the currently rather striking neo-classical edifice was constructed by Benjamin Guinness after he bought two pre-existing Georgian houses in 1862. The story may date back to the earlier houses.

Another rather ornate yet untraceable story, about 'the green lady of St Stephen's Green' can be found in the pages of Padraic O'Farrell's *Irish Ghost Stories*. It describes, in a heavily dramatised style, a young boy growing up in a well-to-do but broken home, with his mother and sister. The boy, David, becomes reclusive and depressed, until he begins having vistations from a 'beautiful lady dressed in green'. His sister Isa, is sceptical, but leaves him alone, to some extent.

David, however has a relapse on meeting his stepfather-to-be. Later that evening he tells his sister that the green lady is going to take him to a 'place where I will always be happy'.

Later that night, Isa awakes to hear a beautiful female voice singing. She goes downstairs, to find the servants muttering about 'the Banshee'.

The next morning, David is found dead, having drowned in the attic water tank.

THE BANSHEE

If one compares the size of Dublin's population with the rest of the country, it would seem the Banshee – Ireland's death messenger – doesn't like the city all that much. However, she does make her occasional appearances, as the previous story attests. For readers interested in the Banshee, probably the definitive text is Patricia Lysaght's 1986 *The Banshee: The Irish Death Messenger*, a remarkable study into the folklore of the *bean sídhe* – Irish for 'fairy woman'. The Banshee is a harbinger of death; if heard *keening* outside people's houses in the dead of night, there's sure to be a death in the family. Banshees are supposed to follow particular names, and the most pure Irish families; an interesting example of nationalism crossing over into the paranormal. This could go some way to explaining the prevalence of the myth in rural areas – Dublin has traditionally been seen as 'more British', while the other areas, especially west of the Shannon River, were regarded as 'more Irish'.

There's no room to delve into this fully here. Lysaght covers the phenomenon, in detail, of how families are 'followed' by the Banshee, including how this list of families changes from county to county, and how the idea of 'follow' may have been something of a mistranslation from Gaelic.

Lysaght interviewed a woman, Anne Hill in Drimnagh, Dublin, on 15 December 1983, who had heard the Banshee the week before on 8 December. An unearthly sound, a 'terrible screaming' had started behind her house. Interestingly, she compared the sound to cats, and decided it wasn't that, 'It was just screaming, screaming like a piercing sort of scream, it just goes on and on and then it gets slower you know … sort of fades away then just fades off and off and off.'

This wasn't the first time that Anne heard the Banshee – she was told by a relative that there was always one person in the family that the Banshee came to.

The next morning, after Anne had heard the Drimnagh Banshee, she received news that her Aunt Jane had died.

THE SANDYFORD BANSHEE

Patrick F. Byrne, in *Tales of the Banshee* – an excellent collection of Banshee folkore – relates a story via his friend, actor Denis Brennan, from around the early twentieth century. According to Brennan's grandmother, inhabitants of Sandyford in south Co. Dublin reported sleepless nights from the 'caterwauling' of the Banshee, which seemed to haunt a haggard belonging to the Pielow family. Mr Pielow, a 'practical man', did not tolerate this situation. Having been woken up by the screaming, he marched to the haggard, armed with a horsewhip.

He found the little woman, and beat her with the whip. She responded by screaming more loudly, and throwing her comb at him (Lysaght reckons that Banshee and mermaid stories have become confused). Pielow managed to chase her out of the haggard, but took ill later that night, and died in his bed.

Byrne also mentions the appearance of a Banshee in Grosvenor Square, in Rathmines.

THE CASTLE GHOSTS

RATHFARNHAM CASTLE

Where's there's a castle, there's bound to be a good ghost story. This book has already covered the poltergeist in Dublin Castle, and the phantom dog of Rathfarnham Castle, but there are others. Rathfarnham Castle's grounds are also said to be haunted the ghost of a boy, 'murdered by a Romany' according to Seymour and Neligan's *True Irish Ghost Stories*. The interior of the castle was haunted by an 'unnerving ghost, who clanked around with his sword, seeking his lady love whose bones had been found and removed from the thick walls. Several of my cousins saw him', wrote Nora Robertson in her book *Crowned Harp*.

The skeleton referred to by Robertson was apparently found in 1880. It was reckoned that the poor woman's remains had been hidden for around 130 years. The story surrounding it is a little hard to believe. Two potential suitors were arguing over the woman's hand in marriage. They decided to fight a duel … but somewhere along the way, she shut herself up behind some wood panelling – or was perhaps locked up there by the two men, in secret. Whoever won the duel would release her, and win her hand. Unfortunately for her, the men succeeded in killing each other, and taking her whereabouts to their graves. An equally doubtful story claims that the lady of the house in 1880 had the corpse's dress made into cushions. Charming!

MALAHIDE CASTLE

The twelfth-century Malahide Castle, alleged to be the oldest inhabited castle in Ireland, harbours some *five* ghosts, according to its official website.

There's fifteenth-century young Lord Galtrim, Sir Walter Hussey, who managed to get married *and* killed in battle on the same day, in 1429. He's said to wander the Castle at night 'pointing to the spear wound in his side and uttering dreadful groans'. It's said that his ghost is annoyed that his young bride married his rival, just as soon as he had 'given up his life in defence of her honour and happiness'. Silly boy.

His wife, Lady Maud Plunkett (*d.*1482), is supposed to haunt the castle too, but appearing just as she looked after her *third* marriage. Maud had become notorious as a 'virago' – a fierce and abusive character who, in death, pursues her third husband throughout the castle. The third ghost, also happens to be this poor man – Chief Baron under Henry VI, John Cornewalsh, 'who merely appears to furnish his spectral spouse with an opportunity of taking a little nocturnal exercise'.

Malahide Castle, which harbours an incredible five ghosts!

Malahide Castle's fourth ghost is reported to be that of Miles Corbett (1595-1662), the Roundhead politician and regicide (he signed Charles I's death warrant), to whom Oliver Cromwell gave the castle and property. Corbett was eventually hung, drawn and quartered in London, but his ghost is seen in various guises at Malahide – riding across the castle grounds, or appearing as a soldier in armour, who then falls into four pieces.

In the sixteenth century, the Talbot family, who inhabited the castle, kept a jester amongst their staff. One of them, known as Puck, 'fell in love with a kinswoman of Lady Elenora Fitzgerald, who was detained at the Castle by Henry VIII because of her rebel tendencies'.

This wasn't the done thing – Puck was found stabbed through the heart, in full costume. Before he died, he promised to haunt the castle 'until a master reigned who chose a bride from the people, but would harm no one if a male Talbot slept under the roof'.

Malahide Castle was sold to the Irish state in 1975 – and Puck is reported to have last appeared in May of the following year, as some of the contents were being sold off by the Talbots. He is said to appear up in old some photographs of the castle, 'one outstanding photograph shows his old bewitching and wrinkled face peering out of the ivy on the wall'.

OTHER CASTLES
A moated Norman castle in Dublin's suburbs, Drimnagh Castle is in good shape, having been restored since the 1980s. Typically it harbours a ghost – that of Eleanora, a woman who apparently threw herself from the battlements after her husband was killed.

In north Co. Dublin, Ardgillan Castle is said to be haunted by a 'woman in white', who apparently haunts the footbridge over the railway that runs between the castle and the sea. The woman is supposed to have committed suicide by drowning herself in the Irish Sea, near Skerries.

The eighteenth-century Magazine Fort in the Phoenix Park is reportedly haunted by the ghost of a British officer. Anyone foolhardy enough to frequent that part of the park at night can apparently see this officer, or at least 'feel his presence'.

Ardgillan Castle is apparently haunted by the ghost of a lady in white that drowned herself in the sea at Skerries. The locals have plenty of stories of this ghostly ilk.

Another 'lady in white' haunts what's left of Castleknock castle, in the grounds of Castleknock College. The story tells of John Tyrrell, of the castle, who abducts Eileen O'Byrne, daughter of a chieftain living on the other side of the river Liffey. Rather than marrying the girl, Tyrell locked her up in the dungeon – where she cut her throat with her broach. A colourful version of this story appears in *History of the Royal Hospital, Kilmainham* by Nathanael Burton, written in 1843.

Strange Goings-on in Dublin 7

The Scoundrel Scaldbrother

The threat of ghostly apparitions are frightening enough, but perhaps even more spine-chilling is the prospect of creatures not quite corporeal – perhaps only partly human, or possessing unearthly talents. London has its uncatchable Springheel Jack; Cornwall its Owlman, and Virginia its Mothman. Dublin's humanoid manifestations are more vague, but worth mentioning because of the fear and hysteria their appearances cause, and their legendary physical abilities. Maybe it's no coincidence that *Dracula*'s author, Bram Stoker, was a Dubliner. The few mentioned here are characters that probably did exist as rather strange humans – but the convolutions of folklore has made them more grotesque and weird.

Scaldbrother, while probably a real, physical person, was a wonderfully named rogue who haunted sixteenth-century Stoneybatter. According to Kevin C. Kearns in *Stoneybatter, Dublin's Inner Urban Village*, Scaldbrother 'roamed the environs accosting people, snatching their possessions, and fleeing with his booty to a vast maze of subterranean passages extending from Smithfield to Arbour Hill. Not only was he a cunning thief, but 'the varlet was so swift of foot as has oftsoon outrun the swiftest and lustiest young men of Osmanstown in the chase'.

Scaldbrother, thus awarded superhuman abilities by the public, would apparently deride his victims – and the pursuing posse, by dashing away to pause by a pub called The Gallows, where he would produce a rope and pretend to hang himself before continuing to 'Scaldbrother's Hole', the entrance to the labyrinth of tunnels.

Despite his near-mythical and superhuman status, Scaldbrother is said to have been eventually caught and hanged, to the delight of many … but his legend has certainly outlived his deeds. According to Kearns, many still hope to find Scaldbrother's lair below Stoneybatter, where his booty is still intact. Let's hope the phantom thief himself isn't still wandering the tunnels.

Billy the Bowl

One of the darker stories that linger in Stoneybatter is that of the eighteenth-century 'Stoneybatter Strangler', thought to have been a man known as 'Billy the Bowl'. Billy was a beggar, born without legs, and had to transport himself in a large wooden bowl, fitted with wheels. He was said to be uncommonly handsome, however, and possessed a mighty pair of arms, which he used to propel himself around, using wooden plugs to grip the cobbles.

At some stage, however, begging wasn't enough for Billy – he decided to use his strength and looks to bring in some large profits so that he could drink and gamble. His first victim was a middle-aged woman. After hiding in some bushes on Grangegorman lane, he started moaning and crying for help as she passed by. She rushed to help, and he overpowered her. Billy made off in his bowl, with the woman's purse – she survived, but was unable to coherently describe the thief.

Billy continued with this manner of robbery for months, and got away with it. Alas, he eventually went too far, strangling a servant girl who struggled too much. The new police force of the time were mobilised, and Billy was forced to lie low. Once the fuss had died down, he returned to his ways, and robbed several more serving girls, causing a permanent patrol to be established in the area. No one ever suspected Billy, the legless man in the bowl.

Finally, Billy met his match. He set himself up in one of his positions again, but this time attracted not one, but two women, both sturdy cooks who were not about to take any nonsense. One of them stuck her hatpin into his eye. His screams attracted the police patrol, and he was arrested. Unfortunately, they could never pin the murder on Billy, but the robberies in Grangegorman certainly came to an end.

THE DOLOCHER

The area of Dublin where High Street meets Thomas Street seems of little consequence now – just a labyrinth of traffic lights and apartments, with a fragment of city wall while St Audoen's church barely getting a look in. In its day, however, Cornmarket was a buzzing area, with a market selling farm produce and animals. The dubious 'sport' of bull-baiting was practiced here – loosing angry pit-bull dogs on a bull, for entertainment purposes. There was also, at one point, a large cage, into which undesirables were thrown – to be pilloried by the public, and to await transportation abroad.

There was also a prison here, known as the Black Dog Prison, or officially, Marshalsea Prison of the Sheriff of the City of Dublin. By 1767 it was one of the oldest buildings in the city, and was in a 'ruinous condition and beyond repair', according to the *Dublin Historical Record*. Newgate prison, built on the north side of the river, beside Green Street, started accepting prisoners.

In 1783 Sir James Fitzpatrick, M.D. wrote, 'The Black Dog in the City of Dublin is in an unwholesome situation in New Hall Market, surrounded with every exhalation necessary to promote putrefaction'. It continued to be used until the 'new' Newgate prison (replacing the 'old' Newgate prison near the Black Dog), was built on the north side of the river, beside Green Street.

Sometime in the late eighteenth century, the Black Dog Prison held a prisoner named Olocher, sentenced to death for committing rape and murder. On the morning of his execution, however, he committed suicide in his cell, robbing the victims of justice, but avoiding the disgrace of being carried on cart to Gallows Green, now Baggot Street, which was then a place of execution.

The next night, a prison sentry who was on duty above a flight of steps leading down into Cook Street was found lying senseless, his gun still by his side. When he came to, one side of his body was unusable, as if he had experienced a stroke. He declared his distress had been caused by the apparition that took the form.

Over the next few nights, the prison sentries saw frightening things, as did the local residents. A night sentry was reported missing – all that he left behind were his clothes and gun. Rumours and terror spread quickly – he had been eaten by the black pig!

The stories became fused, even confused. Olocher, it was said, had turned into a black pig, and was taking his vengeance on the prison guards. He'd 'carried off this last one, body and soul!'

The following day a woman told magistrates under oath that she had seen the *Dolocher*, by which the spectre was now known, going into Christ Church Lane, and that it tried to bite her. It snagged her cloak with its tusks, and she ran in fear, leaving the cloak behind.

The panic went on. A pregnant woman was attacked by the Dolocher, causing her to miscarry. Other women were assaulted, until eventually, no woman would venture out after nightfall, in case

Christ Church Cathedral, Dublin, built in what was the original centre of Viking Dublin – an area full of strange stories, including that of the Dolocher.

Johns Lane, behind Christ Church Cathedral, one of the remaining laneways in the area once known as 'Hell', and surely haunted by the Dolocher.

Schoolhouse Lane, off High Street, where the Dolocher's stolen pigs were hidden.

of being attacked by the porcine demon. It was believed that Olocher's hatred of women tormented him, even after his suicide, and that this made him continue his misdeeds.

A militia was formed to deal with the Dolocher. They roved out from a pub in Cook Street armed with clubs, swords and knives. According to the *The Dublin Penny Journal*, 'such a breaking of legs, fracturing of skulls, stabbing, maiming, and destroying, was never heard of before' – it's not clear how many of these were pigs, and how many were humans. The carcasses of the pigs they did kill vanished overnight from their place of storage, rather mysteriously. However, the Dolocher was not seen again that winter, and the vigilantes were satisfied.

Nevertheless, the Dolocher seems to have returned the following winter, attacking a woman at Fisher's Alley in Wood Quay. People walked the streets in fear.

A blacksmith who lived outside the city, came into Dublin on business one day. Afterwards he had a few drinks with friends, and by the time he was finished, the rain was pelting down. He borrowed a cloak and bonnet from a friend's wife, who said to him 'Take care of the Dolocher!'

She was only half joking. As the blacksmith reached 'Hell' – the yard behind Christ Church, now the City Council offices (see the Ghost Bus section) – he was pounced upon. Not being a small or weak man by any means, he dropped the attacker with one massive blow, shouting: 'Be ye Dolocher or Devil, or what ye may, take that!'

He gave the Dolocher a kick, raising a scream. Standing on his catch, the blacksmith shouted out 'Halloo, halloo, I've killed the Dolocher!'

When the cautious crowd eventually surrounded the two, they discovered that the Dolocher was a man in black pigskin – the same man who had vanished from his sentry post at the Black Dog Prison.

He died of head injuries the next day, but not before he confessed. He had helped Olocher commit suicide, and that the first pig death had given him the idea of for his reign of terror. He was the ringleader behind the killing of all the pigs, and he was the one that stole them too, hiding them in Schoolhouse Lane.

THE SUMMERHILL GHOST

'The Summerhill Ghost' hit the newspapers in January 1966, while workmen were demolishing a crumbling Georgian tenement building in Dublin's north inner city. The house was 118 Summerhill – originally a row of three, but 116 and 117 had already been knocked down. If I've got my location correct, these houses have since been replaced by a high wall, behind which is a Dublin Bus depot.

According to author John J. Dunne, the work stopped when workmen reported an unsettling discovery. They were followed about by a ghostly figure in a butcher's striped apron. A Mr Joseph Byrne told the *Evening Press*:

> I was wrestling with an old stove in the basement when I had a feeling someone was standing behind me, I looked around and saw nothing. After a while the same feeling crept over me and I had another look around. I saw a man, dressed in what appeared to be a butcher's striped jacket, standing looking towards a window. I shouted to the others who were all working above me, but when they came down they couldn't see it at all.

Not that time, perhaps; but two of his co-workers did apparently witness the apparition on other occasions. One of them, a William McGregor, is said to have fainted from the shock.

Oddly enough, when these houses were in their heyday, they were owned and lived in by members of the famous coaching-building Hutton family. One of their surviving creations is the Irish State Coach, built for the British Royal Family, now kept in the Royal Mews at Buckingham Palace. It's most often used by the Queen for the State Opening of Parliament. It got its name not from any declaration of independence or the Irish Free State – but because it was built in 1851 by the then Lord Mayor of Dublin, Mr Hutton.

Somewhere along the way, while the Huttons lived in the row of houses, number 117 gained a reputation for being haunted. According to Dunne, the public's behaviour veered between choosing to 'quicken their pace' when passing by the house, to the gathering of crowds across the street, in case they might see the ghost.

Interestingly, by the time that Mr Byrne and his co-workers saw the butcher ghost in 1966, number 117 had already been knocked down. Dunne spoke to a playwright Patrick Cullen, who based his play *The Dalers* on his experiences in number 116, where he had lived as caretaker.

'The house had a bad reputation for ghosts', Cullen told Dunne. 'Especially the basement, which was certainly considered to be haunted.' He told of reports of 'strange sensations' while climbing the stairs, and 'cold spots' where the temperature seemed to inexplicably drop.

Cullen lived on the top floor. One night he and his wife had some relatives over for a visit. He left the room and crossed the landing to another flat to do something. He had been in the room for several minutes when he heard 'three raps on the door beside him. These were repeated with slow deliberation.'

Cullen assumed it was one of his relatives joking with him. He left the room to find that everyone was sitting in his own flat, just as he had left them.

Dunne wonders if the ghost of 116 and 117 had somehow filtered into 118 after they were demolished. I wonder that if one of the houses was 'haunted', then why not all three? He ends his tale with an offhand, but slightly unnerving conclusion: that 'it is a fact of history that a man named Patrick Conway cut his throat in number 118 Summerhill in 1863. He was a butcher.'

MOUNTJOY SQUARE

Several previous writers on Dublin's hauntings, include Seymour and Neligan, and John J. Dunne, have picked up on the story by a Major Macgregor, who contributed his frightening experiences to a collection called *Real Ghost Stories*, for a journal called *Review of Reviews*, published by W.T. Stead in 1897. Dunne makes a fair assertion that the location of the story is Mountjoy Square. Apart from Rutland Square (now Parnell Square), there are not many places that fit the bill.

Macgregor wrote:

In the end of 1871 I went over to Ireland to visit a relative living in a Square in the north side of Dublin. In January 1872 the husband of my relative fell ill. I sat up with him for several nights, and at last, as he seemed better, I went to bed, and directed the footman to call me if anything went wrong.

I soon fell asleep, but some time after was awakened by a push on the left shoulder. I started up, and said, 'Is there anything wrong?' I got no answer, but immediately received another push. I got annoyed, and said 'Can you not speak, man! and tell me if there is anything wrong.' Still no answer, and I had a feeling I was going to get another push when I suddenly turned round and caught a human hand, warm, plump, and soft. I said, 'Who are you?' but I got no answer. I then tried to pull the person towards me, but could not do so.

I then said, 'I will know who you are!' and having the hand tight in my right hand, with my left I felt the wrist and arm, enclosed, as it seemed to me, in a tight-fitting sleeve of some winter material with a linen cuff, but when I got to the elbow all trace of an arm ceased. I was so astounded that I let the hand go, and just then the clock struck two.

Including the mistress of the house, there were five females in the establishment, and I can assert that the hand belonged to none of them. When I reported the adventure, the servants exclaimed, 'Oh, it must have been the master's old Aunt Betty, who lived for many years in the upper part of that house, and had died over fifty years before at a great age.'

I afterwards heard that the room in which I felt the hand had been considered haunted, and very curious noises and peculiar incidents occurred, such as the bed-clothes torn off, &c. One lady got a slap in the face from some invisible hand, and when she lit her candle she saw as if something opaque fell or jumped off the bed. A general officer, a brother of the lady, slept there two nights, but preferred going to a hotel to remaining the third night. He never would say what he heard or saw, but always said the room was uncanny. I slept for months in the room afterwards, and was never in the least disturbed.

Typical Georgian house Mountjoy Square, where Major Macgregor apparently had his strange experiences.

Mountjoy Square, where Major Macgregor's ghost story seems to have taken place.

THE GHOST BUS

To date I am unaware of any reports of otherworldly Dublin public transport, spiriting the souls of the dead back to their graves in Glasnevin. Instead, the Ghost Bus is a very successful tour run by the city transport company that takes the willing and unsure to visit some of Dublin's darker places – something I'd recommended for resident and visitor alike, if you fancy a hilarious, hair-raising and informative spin of the city any night of the week.

In the last decade, I've taken two Ghost Bus trips; once in 1999 and once in 2007. The tour has changed slightly over the years, moulded by the individual tastes and talents of the tour guides – but it never disappoints. I'd recommend doing the tour in winter, as it departs at around 8p.m., from O'Connell Street. When I first went on board the bus it was summer, and it seemed incongruous to be wandering the city in broad daylight, talking about the dead and undead.

The ghost bus guides also seem to be professional actors; in fact the guide from 2007 was an actor I recognized from a hard-hitting TV drama the week before. Both times, the guides were talented, creative, and knew how to keep a top deck of punters screaming and laughing.

As dusk falls across the Dublin, the Ghost Bus departs, and begins moving along O'Connell Street. At first glance, it looks like every other Dublin double-decker bus, moving through the dwindling traffic. However, the passengers are hidden inside the windows obscured by red velvet curtains, and the sides painted in a faux gothic livery of blues, purples and black illustrations, with a cartoonish ghost. You can't miss it.

As we motor up D'Olier Street, past the old offices of *The Irish Times* that reputedly house a ghost, the guide reels off a list of famous gothic-style writers who had studied in the approaching Trinity College, including Bram Stoker, Sheridan Le Fanu (1814-1873) and Charles Maturin.

Around Trinity and up Nassau Street to Kildare Street, we stop by the College of Physicians. A Dr Samuel Clossey operated his school of anatomy here in the eighteenth century. A 'tall, mean, overbearing' individual, he seems to have eschewed the frivolities of religion and emotion, instead cruelly revelling in shocking his students by slicing up bodies to show that we are little more than meat. Clossey himself met a rather unsavoury end, thanks to his miserliness and bloodthirstiness while 'acquiring' a dead body that had been freshly exhumed and 'sacked up' by some body snatchers. He met his end while trying to manhandle a corpse in through a college window without paying for it, and his ghost is still supposed to wander the college building at night, looking for more human meat to dissect.

The bus drives down Merrion Row, swinging onto Ely Place, where many of Dublin's rich lived: Oliver St John Gogarty (1878-1957) at one time, Bram Stoker's brother Thornley, George Moore (1852-1933) and John 'Black Jack' Fitzgibbon, the Earl of Clare (1746-1802), who lived in Number 6.

The Dublin Ghost Bus. Note lack of driver.

The College of Physicians, Kildare Street, haunted by Dr Clossey.

He is infamously reported to have hung thirteen people in one day (for the sheer hell of it), stating that he would make the Irish as 'tame as castrated cats'.

Oddly enough, the tour guide claims Fitzgibbon was castrated in later years during an 'altercation' in a Turkish brothel, though I haven't found evidence to back this up. In any event, he seems to have survived this setback and died much later at Ely Place. There's an apocryphal story about his funeral; apparently multitudes of Irish commoners carrying sacks joined the funeral cortège. At his graveside the contents of the sacks were thrown onto his coffin: dozens of rotting dead cats. In other variations, the dead cats are thrown during the trip to the cemetery.

During my first Ghost Bus trip, the bus turned back onto Stephen's Green, heading up the east side, formerly known as Monk's Walk, while James, the guide, started ramming a hatpin through a doll wearing a letter 'F'. Down below, Francis, the driver, starts screaming. The 'passengers' are also given a go – some are more 'passionate' about stabbing than others, it seems. This leads into the story of the 7ft (2.13m) tall Lieutenant Jack Hempenstall, a.k.a. 'The Walking Gallows'. Hempenstall hated rebels, and despatched many that he didn't like the look of, by making a noose with his own silk cravat, and swinging the victim over his shoulder, walking around until the poor man expired. According to Peter Somerville-Large's *Irish Eccentrics*, some wit dedicated two lines of verse to the Lieutenant's demise:

Here lies the bones of Hempenstall,
Judge, jury, gallows, rope and all.

A Ghost Bus guide illuminates a box of body-snatched teeth, that he happens to have in his pocket.

The Ghost bus creeps down Long Lane and pulls up to let us out. Our guide is looking shifty and murderous in an overcoat and trilby, carrying a bag of tools and swinging an umbrella as he takes us into St Kevin's Park, formerly known as St Kevin's Cemetery. Standing there in the dark, inside a ruined church, the fine details of the successful theft of a freshly buried body are explained to us in gory detail. The corpse would be impaled under the chin with a hook and pulled from the grave, for sale to the medical community and for the recycling of hair and teeth (wigs and dentures). To the consternation of several people, a box of human teeth is passed around, pulled from some unfortunate mouth in the dark past. According to Dr Fleetwood's book *The Irish Body Snatchers*, George 'Crazy Crow' Hendrick, eighteenth-century day-time 'porter of musical instruments' and 'sack-em-up' also practiced his infamous body snatching skills here

The roofless church, we're told, houses the ghost of Bishop Dermot O'Hurley (*c.*1530-1584), executed for treason, later celebrated as a martyr and beatified by Pope John Paul II as 'Blessed Dermot O'Hurley'. O'Hurley, accused of being part of the Roman Inquisition, was tortured, to force him to embrace Protestantism. He somehow survived this, was executed, and buried in St Kevin's, though the actual location has become lost.

Richard Stanihurst (1547-1618) described the event:

In the Castle Yard, before the officials of the Government, the executioner placed the Archbishop's feet and calves in tin boots filled with oil. They then fastened his feet in wooden shackles or stocks, and placed fire under them. The boiling oil so penetrated the feet and legs that morsels of skin and flesh fell off and left the bones bare. During all his agony the Archbishop gave not a cry, his only expression being 'Jesus, Son of David, have mercy upon me.'

Take note: high season for O'Hurley apparitions is said to be 'late July'. Some of the tourists look extremely uncomfortable here, especially those from 'newer' countries, like the United States, who seemed unused to delving so deep into the past.

The bus then takes us past Marsh's Library, still haunted by Archbishop Marsh, forever searching his books, and the nearby school, dating to 1432, before we are told a tall tale about a premature burial in the grounds of St Patrick's. This is a story that's been told numerous times, and it wanders from place to place; I first heard it connected to Borodale House in Co. Wexford.

A wealthy woman dies, her funeral takes place and she is buried in the family mausoleum, in all her finery. That night one of the funeral attendants (in some versions a family servant) returns to the tomb to steal her jewellery. There's one valuable ring he just can't get wrench from her finger, so he attempts to cut the finger off. As the blood flows, the woman awakes from what is apparently a cataleptic fit, and runs home to her beloved husband, who collapses with shock when he sees her. In some versions he dies on the spot; in others, he takes her back into the home, but they live a cold life, as he believes she is unnaturally back from the grave.

From there the Ghost Bus proceeds past Christ Church Cathedral to St Audoen's church. The area, back in the eighteenth century, was known as 'Hell', which made sense, as it was close to the Four Courts, and surely housed dozens of young barristers engaged in 'devilling', or apprenticed to a senior barrister — these young lawmen were known as 'devils'. In any case, a sign of the time supposedly read:

To Rent: Rooms in Hell. Lawyers Preferred.

St Audoen's church, where Darkey Kelly is said to have given up her child.

In eighteenth-century Dublin, a brothel stood there: the Maiden Tower, on Fishamble Street. Nowadays the City Council buildings dominate the area, overshadowing even Christ Church Cathedral. On Fishamble Street stands a bar called Darkey Kelly's, named after the madame of the Maiden Tower. It seems that one of her most regular customers was Simon Luttrell – not only a member of the Hellfire Club, but also none other than the City Sheriff. Darkey seems to have looked after Luttrell a little too well – before long, she was pregnant with his child.

This is where the story gets a little confusing. In one version, Kelly brings the baby to the side door of nearby St Audoen's church, to give it up for adoption, I presume. Given the health facilities available to the average person in eighteenth-century Dublin, it would hardly be surprising for a child to die at birth; yet Kelly seems to have been arrested and tried for the murder of the child, despite no body ever being found. It's no coincidence that Luttrell, desperate to save face, was himself the prosecutor of the trial. It was a daring and chancy move – but her accusations towards him must have been seen as the rantings of madwoman. After all, what would the City Sheriff been doing, dallying with a prostitute?

The bus makes a stop at the back gate to St Audoen's, which is also an original city gate. It's at a door, off a curving set of steps, that Kelly is supposed to have left the baby. Apparently the ghost of a woman in black – with black hair – can be seen roaming these steps on a dark night, looking for her child.

According to Terry O'Hagan, who has worked as a guide in St Audoen's, numerous local people maintain that they were always warned away from the steps as children, because of the ghost of a 'green lady' who appeared there. Some versions of the story, in its modern telling, seem to connect Darkey

'The Hellfire Club', the spooky hunting lodge in the Dublin Mountains, home to eighteenth-century 'divilment' of the highest order.

Kelly to this apparition. While this seems pretty logical – the steps don't seem large enough to accommodate two female wraiths – the story could also be a simple cautionary tale to keep children safe from more corporeal dangers.

Numerous other stories and legends are attached to these steps – and to the church of St Audoen's. In the eighteenth century, a gang known as the Liberty Boys made up of weavers from the Pimlico part of the nearby Liberties area, would engage in bloody street wars with the Ormonde Boys – butchers from the bank of the Liffey. Apparently, after a nasty skirmish, the butchers would leave the bodies of dead weavers hanging from the archway picture above.

Inside the church, stands the 'Lucky Stone' – said to being luck to anyone who touches it. Whatever about being lucky, it's definitely well travelled; it arrived in St Audoen's in the fourteenth century, having possibly been a boundary stone at the early Christian settlement where St Patrick's Cathedral now stands, but later ended up standing outside St Audoen's. Anyone passing it – on the way up or down the steps – would be drawn to touch it. It was a great way of drawing people towards the church; an unscrupulous politician realised this, and 'moved' the stone to a nearby fountain that he had commissioned in Cornmarket, in order to boost his popularity in the run up to an election. The Lucky Stone was stolen in the early nineteenth century, and vanished for years – before popping up again two decades later. According to nineteenth-century historian John T. Gilbert, it spent some time outside adjacent Catholic church of St Audoen's built during the 1840s, following the beginning of Catholic Emancipation. The Lucky Stone is now inside a twentieth-century church porch, next to the tower, where quite a legend has grown up around it. The stone is said to glow, shake, jump, groan, get heavier and even take human form if anyone attempts to steal it.

The last time I took the Ghost Bus Tour, the guide suggested that we all take photographs while standing on these steps in the dark – using our camera flashes. He reckoned that it being such a haunted place that we may well capture 'orbs'. Many succeeded – there were many gasps of wonder from up and down the steps. Accepted by some people as 'evidence' of the paranormal, in fact they're simply circular artifacts in photographs, caused by the flash illuminating dust particles, or more typically in Dublin, *rain droplets*.

For more about the Ghost Bus, please visit www.dublinbus.ie/sightseeing

GIANT RATS IN BOOTERSTOWN

While not really a ghost story, I felt this had to be included as a finale to *Haunted Dublin* – if only to disturb anybody who happens to be reading this while travelling on the southside section of Dublin's DART train service.

It's a story that turns up Weston St John Joyce's 1912 *The Neighbourhood of Dublin*, concerning an apparent rodent problem in eighteenth-century Dublin suburbia:

> *Walsh's Impartial News Letter* of 16 May 1729 contains the following curious item of news in regard to this neighbourhood: –'This morning we have an account from Merian that a parcel of these outlandish Marramounts which are called Mountain Rats who are now here grown very common … walk in droves and do a great deal of mischief.' The story then relates how these mysterious pests devoured a woman and a nurse-child in Merrion and that the inhabitants 'killed several which are as big as Katts and Rabbits … This part of the country is infested with them. Likewise we hear from Rathfarnham that the like vermin destroyed a little Girl in the Fields.

Bibliography
and further reading

Barrington, J., *Personal Sketches and Recollections of His Own Times*, 1827.

Blather.net: The Hellfire Club (http://blather.net/blather/the_hellfire_club).

Byrne, P. F., *Tales of the Banshee* (Mercier: Cork, 1987).

Byrne, P., *Irish Ghost Stories* (Mercier: Cork, 1965).

The Dublin Penny Journal, 'The Dolocher (a legend of the Black Dog Prison, Dublin)' vol. 1, Number 22, 24 November 1832.

Dames, M., *Mythic Ireland* (Thames & Hudson: London, 1996).

Dunne, John J., *Haunted Ireland* (Appletree Press: Belfast, 1977).

Early Irish Myths and Sagas (Penguin Classics: London, 1981).

Fleetwood, J., *The Irish body Snatchers, a history of body snatching in Ireland* (Tomar, 1988).

Griffin, V., *Mark of Protest* (Gill & Macmillan: Dublin, 1993).

Holzer, H., *The Lively Ghosts of Ireland* (Random House: London, 1967).

The Irish Digest, 'The Case of the Stoneybatter Strangler', July 1964.

Joyce, J., *Finnegans Wake*, 1939, Part: 3 Episode: 14.

Joyce, W. St J., *The Neighbourhood of Dublin* (Gill & Macmillan: Dublin, 1977).

Lysaght, P., *The Banshee: The Irish Death Messenger* (O'Brien Press: Dublin, 1986).

Kearns, K. C., 'The Scoundrel Scaldbrother', *Stoneybatter, Dublin's Inner Urban Village*,(Glendale: 1989).

Malahide Historical Society, *Malahide Castle Spooks*, Newsletter No. 32.

McManus, D., *The Middle Kingdom: The Faerie World of Ireland* (Colin Smythe: Buckinghamshire, 1959).

Moylan, T. K., 'The Little Green Dublin Prison', *Dublin Historical Record*, Vol. VIII, No. 3 June-August, 1946.

O'Farrell, P., *Irish Ghost Stories* (Gill & Macmillan: Dublin, 2004).

Pritchett, V.S., *Dublin*, (Bodley Head: London, 1991).

Robertson, N, *Crowned Harp* (Allen Figgis: Dublin, 1960).

Seymour, J., and Neligan, H., *True Irish Ghost Stories* (Senate 1926).

Somerville-Large, P., *Irish Eccentrics* (Lilliput Press: Dublin, 1975).

Watkins, A., *The Old Straight Track* (Abacus, 1925).